The
Dharma *of*
Direct Experience

The
Dharma *of*
Direct Experience

NON-DUAL PRINCIPLES
OF LIVING

A Sacred Planet Book

PAUL WEISS

Inner Traditions
Rochester, Vermont

Inner Traditions
One Park Street
Rochester, Vermont 05767
www.InnerTraditions.com

Text stock is SFI certified

Sacred Planet Books are curated by Richard Grossinger, Inner Traditions editorial board member and cofounder and former publisher of North Atlantic Books. The Sacred Planet collection, published under the umbrella of the Inner Traditions family of imprints, includes works on the themes of consciousness, cosmology, alternative medicine, dreams, climate, permaculture, alchemy, shamanic studies, oracles, astrology, crystals, hyperobjects, locutions, and subtle bodies.

Cataloging-in-Publication Data for this title is available from the Library of Congress

ISBN 978-1-64411-533-6 (print)
ISBN 978-1-64411-534-3 (ebook)

Printed and bound in the United States by Lake Book Manufacturing, Inc. The text stock is SFI certified. The Sustainable Forestry Initiative® program promotes sustainable forest management.

10 9 8 7 6 5 4 3 2 1

Text design and layout by Virginia Scott Bowman
This book was typeset in Garamond Premier Pro with Gill Sans and Bookman used as the display typefaces

To send correspondence to the author of this book, mail a first-class letter to the author c/o Inner Traditions • Bear & Company, One Park Street, Rochester, VT 05767, and we will forward the communication, or contact the author directly at **info@thewholehealthcenter.org**.

Contents

PART TWO
When Our Life Becomes the Path

Memos to Myself

Note to the reader

This book discusses various aspects of non-duality and the wisdom traditions. While reading, you may find it useful to refer to the list of terms relevant to this book and their associated meanings, located in the final chapter titled "Useful Terms."

All Reality Begins with this Moment of Experience

*W*e sit together in the late day, as the sun is passing. We are at rest, and there is a shared heartbeat between us. A shared recognition of consciousness in our eyes. We have relaxed into what is fundamental to our being: the harmonizing field of the heart, the coherence of the present, the surrender of distraction and self-consciousness. Absent our self-centered mental worlds, awareness is simply a light that allows this moment's own transparency to energy and form and emptiness; to the sighing of the sunset fields. And to the undefined reality of You and I awake to each other, which is only the universe's latest recognition and celebration of itself.

Yet how often are we locked into our thoughts of past and future, near and far, theory and explanation, fears and plans; thoughts of he said/she said, thoughts of better and worse, thoughts of self, thoughts of previous thoughts? What do they have in common? They are all thoughts. They are all an imaginary film in which we live most of our lives, in which awareness spends its time like a lost child in someone else's movie, beholden to the script.

When awareness returns to itself, rests in its own luminous nature and its home in emptiness, reality is wide open. Now the passing day turns from the early gloaming, the gentle and still sparkling wash of post-sunset pinks and peacocks and gold-lined grays; and the blue hour begins, slowly darkening into purple and black. But there is nothing fixed, nothing solid, here. There is awareness. This wash of color and form, these transformations of the air, are the transparent shades of an infinite moment; the darkening woods are a lover of infinite space and depth. Now there is a screech, now a rustle. The single note of a bird— or a wind chime—or a distant car. Or a heartbeat. Or of love recognizing itself once again.

Reality begins with this moment of awareness. Where else will it arise? Will it be the reality of the film or the reality of open sky and deep woods; the reality of the dream images or the reality of empty awareness; the reality that beckons newly and infinitely to us, or the reality that is already prescribed? It begins here, in the moment of shadows, and in the sunrise.

When awareness recognizes and relaxes in its own openness, it *illuminates* all arising content without grasping or labeling, without pushing it away. When awareness does not recognize its own nature, its own openness, it is instead *hypnotized* by the arising content. This is like the tug of the cart pulling the horse: awareness *identifies* with all the random or pre-conditioned contents, thoughts, representations, and projections of the mind that every moment drag us, and structure our experience in fixed ways. In this state, we may believe whatever is on the "television," in which even the present moment is seen through the screen of our mental representation.

This latter state is the world as we routinely know it—with our experience prescribed for us. This is called normal. It is our default, or "automatic," setting. We may even say it is our "sleep" setting. However, if we are able to withdraw our attention from the screen, we may re-allow a receptive openness to the field of experience right now, neither pre-conceived nor pre-judged. This choice often requires a conscious "manual setting." This openness of attention is available to any of us any time, and may be practiced.

This faculty of openness obviously serves us by allowing a more present, spontaneous, and creative response to our everyday experience and to each other. It is also the beginning of what we may call *contemplative* openness, when the awareness is allowed to remain in a state of relaxed and receptive presence. It is not a static presence, but one which has an active and genuine interest in understanding—opening to—the truth of things; an interest which does not enlist the mind's cleverness or projections. Rather, it relies on a deeper organ of listening, or receptive awareness, that is more coherent than the perseverations of the mind. Then, this moment emerges as an infinite sea of possibility and revelation that opens itself to us in accordance with our availability; that is, in accordance with our own willingness and capacity to open to *it*. It will disrobe for us layer by layer to reveal its naked body and its heart—insofar as we gradually disrobe from our layers of mental preoccupation and conditioning.

Here we have the invitation and the opportunity to drop through many layers of externality, separation, projection, and identification with our personally and culturally inherited ways of defining reality. It is simply an intent and sincere listening into the heart of this moment. This is both the cultivated field of our openness, and, we might say, the growing "static electricity," in which the lightning of revelation, of sudden illumination, may strike. We may say that our growing coherence gives way to our transparency. That is how it works. And then we know something directly about the intimate nature of reality—however paradoxical to consensus reality—with an authority and confidence that all the other mental faculties are not capable of.

It is naturally difficult to make the small, sustained choices of attention that enable us, over time, to rest in that open field. Our attention has been trained—like a kidnap victim—to identify with its mental captors, and won't walk out the front door. Or—to reverse the image— imagine you are standing in the doorway of a treasure house, which is the spacious home of your true being. Outside, bullhorns are blaring, and a political parade is passing by, complete with clowns, music, special-interest floats, and dancing animals. Finally comes the politician on his loudspeaker, promising you anything and asking for your vote.

You can't help but be engaged by all the activity. Your attention remains outside.

The parade represents all the contents of your mind. The politician signifies all the ways your mind has learned to describe, organize, and judge reality. It will promise you anything—pleasure, freedom, approval—and assure you it is your only hope, if you will just stick with it. It also gives you endless content for your attention. That parade of the mind is constant, and our loyalty to its activity and projections is habitual. Consequently, even the present moment of experience is largely seen through its blare and glare.

Alternately, starting at this same moment of experience—the same doorway—your attention leaves the parade and turns back into the open space of your home. This is sometimes referred to as "looking within"—but the "within" is not a closed-off place. It is not inside you, or inside your mind. Rather, it simply means looking within—or opening to—the nature of this moment, and the spacious nature of your own awareness, before the mind gets its hands on it.

The depth and fullness of the world lie in what we do not routinely see or feel, and have forgotten. But this knowing is not only about the physical form and texture of things—it is also a deep seeing into, and through, the world of appearances itself, to palpate the living flesh beneath the skin of our projections and concepts. It is like palpating the warm flesh of non-duality through the cold skin of separateness. It is a relaxation in awareness. It is the receptive attention that allows the more holistic truth of this moment to reveal itself to our deeper organ of knowing. We may truly call it our "home," because we can only be truly at home in this moment, and in this space, of being. And we may call it a treasure house because the treasures of being are revealed here in this space of receptive knowing.

It is naturally easier for our active and projective mind to be drawn to the outside activity, to the parade. After all, the parade offers so many things to focus on. Whereas at home, there appears to be nothing—only openness, or emptiness. It is only when the mind comes to discover that its own true nature *is* openness that the resting in openness becomes easy and pleasurable. But in contemplative openness, we can directly experience the realm of awareness and its content without our preconceptions or assumptions. In that place of openness, even the categories of *self* and *other* cease to arise. The categories of *everything* or *nothing* may cease to arise. And certainly the mind's projections and reactions to the various contents of awareness cease to arise. Hence, we begin to experience one harmonious presence in which awareness and its contents rest together as one luminous space that is not otherwise divided or defined. Awareness may relax and open to its field of experience until its inherent and interpenetrating love and unity are revealed.

This is the context in which the shifts in experience described in this book have occurred. They may happen spontaneously, as many people have testified, apart from any formal or deliberate practice. The "shift" cannot be contrived or "accomplished" by anyone. It arises as a slip, an accident in consciousness, in a moment when our separative scaffolding can no longer be sustained. But, as many have said, meditation—contemplative openness—makes us more accident-prone.

Although my own tendencies, and ongoing practice from an early age, predisposed my availability to the experiences that I recount and comment on in this book, they are potentially available to all. They constitute the greater landscape, or context, of all the other personal landscapes we each choose to become absorbed in; and that greater landscape becomes apparent only as we relax our preoccupation with our manufactured landscapes for a while.

I think of when I was a boy and would travel with my parents on long camping trips up through New England, into the maritime provinces of Canada, and elsewhere. As we traveled through this countryside, my parents would continually comment on how beautiful the landscape was. But my brother and I survived these long car trips by burying ourselves in comic books in the back seat. My parents would express dismay that we were not enjoying what was outside the car window. But we had more compelling and stimulating landscapes for our attention—the landscapes of comic books. I can remember fleeting glimpses of the countryside , but I did not choose—I was not naturally ready—to make it part of my story. Yet the actual landscape was always equally there for me; and, of course, I later came to love it. The landscape I describe herein is also always in the background for all of us, though the prevailing landscapes of the mind are usually too compelling.

But *that* landscape will be there for each of us when all the other landscapes are gone. It is what we are.

letting my eyes go
soft, I stopped turning
things into objects

When Nothing Experiences Itself as Everything

Nothing has been experiencing itself as everything for longer than everything can remember—for as long as No Thing has appeared as Every Thing. The Indian sage, Meher Baba, once put it this way: "In the beginning, delighting in the nature, or Truth, of Infinite Being, God asked, 'Who am I?' And all of creation manifested as the answer to the question; namely, 'I am God.'" In whatever language we would like to put it, the question and the answer, the everything and the nothing, are One. From an eternal standpoint, the oneness of the question and the answer is true in an absolute moment—or in any moment. From the standpoint of time, the answer to God's question unfolds as an evolution and display of energy and matter, form and consciousness.

As an expression of that same consciousness, we also ask questions. And it would appear that the same Truth is intent and capable of knowing itself through us; not only *indirectly,* through our mental faculties, but also *directly,* as a direct awakening to itself. When, in our questioning, we simply sit with openness and intention upon the truth, our intention corresponds with God's. And when we genuinely ask, "Who am I?" we are asking God's question, and holding space for the answer.

Our species has inherited a lot of intellectual and spiritual history, the sum accumulation of logic, insight, analysis, speculation, fear, bright spring mornings, and bad digestion. A significant part of this history also comes from apparent moments of direct seeing—a largely latent faculty that allows for unusually integrated perceptions that are not entirely limited by the structures of our conceptual, analytical, or sense apparatus. These direct perceptions, however, are naturally reduced to forms of expression that reflect the language, the intellectual possibilities, and even the cultural pressures of the age.

We can each probably point to our visionary heroes or heroines, past and present—sages, visionaries, and poets within various religious traditions, or outside these traditions altogether—whose testimonies have a ring of truth for us, and inspire our understanding and even our behavior. These testimonies seem to point beyond the normally separative activities and prejudices of the mind to a more open, integrated, playful, and loving discernment of "who we are" and "what this is." These are testimonies that support our own capacity to pay loving and appreciative attention to life and to those around us, while we slowly free ourselves from the more narrow, exclusive, or reactive sides of our nature.

Steve Gaskin once speculated on the normal bell curve of the possibilities of human experience, concluding that because the number of people living on the planet today equals the number of all people living throughout history, that same bell curve of experience across human history exists in its entirety right now. That essentially means that the equivalent of Rumi, Shakyamuni Buddha, St. Francis, Mirabai, Hildegard, Chuang-tse, St. Teresa of Avila, Black Elk, and the Baal Shem Tov are alive today—as is every deluded, genocidal tyrant. Moreover, many of us live in an increasingly liberal intellectual culture that is cross-fertilized by all past spiritual traditions, allowing an open and unaffiliated field for exploration and expression of spiritual truth. Even the great rationalist pursuit of science is coming around full circle to articulate the essence of mystical experience.

It is no surprise, therefore, that we are experiencing a kind of springtime of spiritual exploration and testimony, with many teachers coming forth with various degrees of realization, complemented by a growing demand for such teachers. Many of these teachers have trained within, and inherited, the wisdom lineages of the great traditions, and convey the reliability and credibility of these traditions—as well as some of the baggage and blind spots. Some of these teachers have trained in the traditions but have also developed in unique directions. And still others have testified to their personal, spontaneous, and well-founded experience of insight, not based on training within the traditions, but certainly able to draw on these traditions.

This leaves us as a culture both rich and somewhat confused, which is inevitable when we don't have one ingrained tradition setting the gold standard of truth. It leaves us, especially in a consumer culture, window shopping for tastes of experience to feather our caps, enhance our lifestyles, or, of course, relieve our suffering—uncertain of our opportunity, or even of our motivation, for a deepening clarity of practice. But our time is indeed rich with possibility.

I was born into a slightly earlier moment of this cultural progression, coming of age in the sixties, when the very first Zen masters and lamas from afar were slowly introducing themselves to American culture. (Of course, there were isolated earlier visits from the East a century ago.) I was raised in a barely Jewish, atheistic, humanistic tradition in New York City—providing a viewpoint I somehow took for granted, even as I was drawn from early childhood toward mystical teachings and intuitions. Psychology and mythology were both part of that fascination. I first read Joseph Campbell at thirteen and had inexplicable dreams and longing for Tibet, read R. M. Bucke's *Cosmic Consciousness* at fourteen, along with Whitman and the Christian mystics, read Einstein at fifteen, and Zen at sixteen. Much of this I describe in the opening chapter.

Zen was my foundational training, and Buddhist thought and practice is as basic as anything in my make-up. The full spectrum of Buddhist insight, wisdom, and compassion has always seemed to me to well account for the deepest totality of conscious and super-conscious experience. I especially appreciated the teachings of the *Nyingma* tradition of Tibetan Buddhism, the writings of the sage Longchenpa, and the direct non-dual meditation and teachings of *dzogchen* practice. In my later years, I was delighted to encounter the classical Chinese *Hua-yen* school of thought, which to my mind is the most profound and complete philosophical articulation and confirmation (if needed) of the timeless *dharmadhatu,* the non-dual interpenetrating totality of being of which I had been given a glimpse.

But that language is just my particular proclivity, and none of it precludes or excludes my deep love for, and adoption of, the other transmissions of truth. After all, the mystical embrace of Allah (or *Alaha* or *Elohim*) is equally interpenetrating and revelatory. As I have written elsewhere, all language, including all spiritual language, is poetry. And every poetry, and every language—by its basic culture and structure—has its own genius for perceiving, engaging, and expressing reality. Our different languages cross-pollinate and mutually enhance the dimensions of our understanding, and open us to new experiences, and new dimensions of ourselves, without being contradictions. This is not only true for the transmission of the Christian passion, for example, and for the keen and uplifted heart and vision of the Sufis, but also for the indigenous languages that get into the bones of the Earth—and where we can find profound images and echoes of the radical, interpenetrating metaphysics of *Hua-yen.* They are all windows into the totality of universal experience—which, in turn, are clouds and mists, mountains and rivers without end, the rise and fall of empires and breath, gum on the pavement, raven's flight. So, perceiving all of the teachings as nested within each other, and within the all-inclusive truth of this moment, I have never been strongly inclined to call myself a "Buddhist." (Which is, of course, a very Buddhist stance.)

I do often speak as a Buddhist, however, because I find that the direct phenomenological nature of Buddhist language, and its embodied practice, come naturally to me, and more easily serves as a technical and unencumbered teaching language, and as a *lingua franca* between different contemplative languages, non-dual perspectives, science, and personal and transpersonal psychology. But for me it is not a closed system, by any means. I am, at the same time, very easy with my use of the word "God." It does not reflect a preference for any theology over Buddhist metaphysics, but rather a deep appreciation of both poetries; and the need for both, if I am to speak from the heart. "God" carries the weight of my own intimate experience of, and dialogue with, the fundamental nature of reality. I tell anyone uncomfortable with the word that they can take it as an acronym for the Great Originating Dynamic (or the Grand Old Dance).

It is largely a matter of language. If we say that God is another name for Conscious Loving Presence, or for the empty, awake, and responsive holographic nature of reality, then it is equally fair to say that all of that is only another word for God. Because there is an infinite relationship between ourselves and that which is infinite, whether we approach our path as an awakening to God—or as an awakening of our Buddha-mind and our Buddha-heart—is, from a practical standpoint, a matter of how our acquired mental impressions in this life have led to our initial preference for how we address, love, and engage reality. This is not about "mix and match" spirituality, however. It is still about the strength and coherence of our dedication to a selfless reality that fuses the integrity of our practice. Nevertheless, you may find in my writing a frequent idiosyncratic shifting of language—as if a rogue word processor began randomly shifting fonts within a given text, yet always conveying the same information.

My studies and influences have ranged widely. I was naturally attracted to the teachings of Bhagavan Ramana Maharshi. (I recall walking up Upper West Side Broadway at age nineteen, on my way to the Zen center, holding a mantra I had given myself: "No more games, Bhagavan.") I was, at a later point, deeply touched by *A Course in Miracles*. And, much earlier, I was affected most profoundly and extensively by the early teachings of that remarkable individual known in those days as Bubba or Da Freejohn, whose teachings I have probably internalized more that I even realize, and one of whose most succinct pronouncements, "Persist as love despite all evidence to the contrary," I have made my own to this day.

Much of my earliest foundational experience is addressed in the next chapter. This leaves, as the later foundational pieces of my life's trajectory, my long history of practice in the *shabd yoga* and *Sant Mat* lineage of teachings (see the chapter titled "In the Arc of the Fountain"); my training and experience with emotional integration work (see "The Pterodactyl"); and the work of Charles Berner, who developed the process that came to be known as "the Enlightenment Intensive." In my own work, I changed its name to "the True Heart, True Mind Intensive," which was truer to my own outlook, and was, for me, less commodifying. This profoundly conceived process integrates contemplation with communication in a way that amplifies the awakening power of both. I have been running True Heart, True Mind Intensive retreats since the early eighties, and some of my own deepest experience has occurred when I myself have been a participant in such retreats.

Finally, my early study of *tai chi ch'uan,* which began in New York in 1967, eventually led to my extensive involvement, here and in China, with *qigong* and the Taoist lineage of teachings—which, as I have come to integrate them with my other practices, have also contributed to a transparency of body and spirit.

If these biographical details, and those that follow, conjure up any image of fabled autobiography—forget it. When you place those mere details in the context of an actual ordinary and messy life—marriage, kids, work, bills, and the standard thousand and one opportunities for misguided behaviors and uneducated choices—it seems less exceptional and more familiar. None of the exotic details are ever really the point. Perhaps the only real lesson to be learned from any bio, however it looks, is that of a certain single-mindedness; that is, the clarifying of priorities and the quality of intention, as well as the continued willingness to question or undermine our conditioning on behalf of the truth.

All of which can keep us from foundering forever in the circus of distraction and false promise.

Our lucid experiences can ground us and make us more capable of and committed to acting clearly. But the dance of life will stir up many eddies in the mind that cloud the windshield. Just as with nighttime driving, the onrushing glare of bright headlights can be quite challenging—dangerously disorienting, perhaps, to the inexperienced driver. But, with experience, we learn how to inwardly shelter ourselves from the glare, not give it our full attention, look slightly down and to the side, and use the right edge of the road as our reference point. The onrushing headlights of the mind can offer a similar disorienting glare. But we learn not to give it our full and serious attention, and to keep confidence in a certain inner reference point along the right side of the road. Of course, for that moment, the easy clarity of the road is obscured. However, we each have an inner gyroscope or homing device that we must, at any given point, activate in the midst of our outer circumstances—and it will open before us the appropriate path of surrender and of practice.

I did in fact marry and "raise" six kids, who are still much a part of my life, along with ten grandchildren. I am frequently buoyed by the depth of their humanity and spirit. And to speak of what I owe my erstwhile partner, Alexandra, who is now passed, could be a whole other book. There is no "spiritual" substitute for the growth that comes from a relationship to another human being. The lessons I learned, and the passionate, and sometimes bracing, teaching and cross-pollinating of understanding that she gifted me, were exactly the gifts I needed for who I was to become. Whenever I have occasion to think, "Gee, I'm grateful for learning that lesson back then, so I don't have to learn it now," it was likely from Alex that I learned it.

I was also lucky to be able to choose work that reinforced and reminded me of, rather than distracted me from, my deepest intentions and need to practice. Founding The Whole Health Center in Bar Harbor in 1981 offered me a broad palette for serving, teaching, and learning, and for developing a comprehensive vision. As all the areas of my work and practice have continued to integrate and coalesce, they have also led to a desire to write—with one book out, and several in the (sometimes dysfunctional) creative pipeline.

During a rare vacation a few winters ago, on a remote island in the southern Bahamas, I found myself sitting on a high coral outcrop at the edge of a deserted cove. Meditating under a scrubby tree, just out of the hot sun, and with a cool ocean breeze blowing from behind me, there suddenly blew across my mind the thought to write this book. It had never been my expectation, intention, or presumption to write about the details of my own spiritual experience. In fact, it had never occurred to me before; whereas there were other books, I thought, waiting to be written. Now, it seemed, it was obviously what I was supposed to do.

Up until now I had presumed to speak and write on the basis of my collective experience, including a lifetime's living, working, practicing, and studying. And, more importantly, with the authority of those direct occasions of revelation. But I had never given much attention to making an account of, or much reference to, those most intimate experiences themselves. (In fact, just recently, when discovering a recording of an online interview I did in 2011, I was surprised to hear myself all but denying them.) Suddenly it seemed that they were the treasures that needed to be unfolded, or unpacked, in detail. They were, after all, the most essential experiences of my life, and the foundation of anything else I had to say. And in this most transitory—and closer to ending—lifetime, it now seemed my most important piece of business was to record them. (Three of these experiences—see "On the Subway," "Dancing at a Festival," and "Neither Life nor Death"—have also been commented on in my previous book, *Moonlight Leaning Against an Old Rail Fence—Approaching the Dharma as Poetry*.)

Not only did I owe it to the world to make a direct account, but I also owed myself the challenge of recording that account; that is, of making the clearest possible articulation of what is often spoken of in generalities or formulaic references. There is no vainglory when I say,

"I owe it to the world." I believe every life simply owes back the best fruits of its own experience, to become the very best and most serviceable compost we can become, in keeping with our own nature, as we disappear back into the life of the whole. As my nature, in the broad sense, is that of a poet, this was one of the poems I owed leaving behind.

Although my experiences are not common, neither are they special. Many among us have had direct realizations, revelations that bypass the routine avenues and structures of the mind. And I have been privileged to be there on that occasion for others. I am not, after all, speaking of anything new; but each articulation, if it is based on recording a direct experience, may always have something new to offer. When I read the accounts and the accomplishments of the great masters, or the depth and lucid straightforwardness of their teachings, of course I think: "Who am I to say anything? I am just a foolish (seventy-five-year-old) kid." But that same foolish kid, finding a beautiful pebble on the beach, wouldn't hesitate to bring it home and share it for what it is. I can at least make a humble effort to be faithful to the truth of what I have been shown directly—with no further claims—and my elders in spirit may kindly receive the pebble and smile indulgently and place it on the shelf. Or some other fool might crack open the pebble to find all the teachings revealed once again. Indeed, it is just that a fool can see these things that testifies to the all-pervasive mercy and accessibility of the dharma, and to its immediate accessibility to other fools.

I only intended so much in this writing: to document a limited portion of my direct experience, offer a glimpse of the "big view," and present and clarify a certain understanding of reality based on that experience—inspiring others, perhaps, with my own testimony. In part one I chose to record only those experiences that still live in me as thoroughly revelatory. In other words, they showed me something directly and authoritatively that I could not have claimed to know with authority a moment before; that the mind by itself can never know with authority. But on these occasions, a veil is torn away such that reality simply knows itself.

Part two of this book grew unexpectedly as a means to further highlight some of the practical implications of part one and to pull together pieces of the broad spiritual picture with the intimate and tender details of our human psychology—the mechanisms of the ego and brain/mind functioning that define, inhibit, and also enable our full spiritual development. It became a bit more elaborate than its original intention, and yet it still does not do full justice to the ideas that are raised—to which I intend to return in future writings. But if this book is able to affirm, instruct, or inspire a new level of integration, understanding, or foundation for our practice together as human beings, then I will be grateful.

As in much of my writing, there tends to be a continuous shuttle between the personal, the poetic, and the didactic (which I hope is not a dirty word). Certain themes or ideas seem to reiterate themselves throughout the book; and, to an extent, each chapter reflects and recasts all the others. I chose to leave the reiterations, hoping that they serve to make certain new concepts more familiar and accessible, rather than merely repetitious.

The experiences in part one all seem to reinforce one common experience of reality. Understandably. For they are each glimpsing the same landscape through different windows, or through interchangeable depths of perspective. And they might easily have occurred in a different sequence. But the writing also made me aware of some of the themes in my own early development that were, in some way, archetypal of the journey itself. The crucial factors in becoming open to insight are always present in each person's journey, uniquely situated in each life. For someone else, these realizations will occur in wholly different circumstances. But they are important passages in the journey of consciousness, and so I have recorded some of them in the first chapter of this book.

Thus, there is an element of spiritual autobiography. However, the focus is not on my life, but on the unfolding of understanding. This understanding belongs to the world as part of that emergent evolution that Pierre Teilhard de Chardin might call "christic," and the sage Robert Sardello might call "sophianic," and Zen might call the cypress tree in the garden. Even then, there is a significant piece left out: the nuts and bolts of life, and the trials, training, enlightenment, and steam cleaning of life in the world, and life in relationship. I acknowledge the limited scope of the personal account. It does not go into the details of the struggles of my individual humanity, which might also be edifying. That would have been a much more momentous task. Nor is it, though, meant to promote a one-sided view of myself. It is meant to be an affirmation of, and a testament to, the deeper reality that holds all of us, even as we work through our individual karmas.

While it is to be hoped and reasonably expected that the depth of spiritual experience is consistent with the growing emotional maturity, psychological insight, behavioral and relational skills, and overall discernment and integration of our lives, these are domains that require their own fierce commitment and learning curve. Though many spiritual insights and experiences are inherently integrative in their effect on daily life, this is not always so. Their own integration, and their greater integrative effect, is more likely assured, however, if we have made an equal commitment to being honest and humble disciples of life's lessons, humiliations, demands, failures, and restructuring of our egoic characters. It is life itself that knows how to work and soften the material, and find its enlightening way into the cracks, whether we are living in a monastery or in a traditional household. Life is messy. We may do very well avoiding the mess, but that is likely to leave something unintegrated. We needn't be shy of the messiness of life, nor shy nor judgmental about the messiness of the "self." There is a technical Sanskrit phrase for this: "the whole enchilada."

When one tells a dream that hasn't been told, one remembers things that would have otherwise been lost from recollection. When one describes an experience that has not been fully described, one mines treasures that were never fully mined. May the gifts of both tellings go to the glory of the Mother Lode.

PART ONE

Tripping over the Light

The light is everywhere, but, miraculously, people rarely trip over it. But, now and again, you find a real klutz. *I myself have been known to be such a klutz.*

RAV SHMUEL PINCHAS HALEVAI (APOCRYPHAL)

Someone Does

Sometimes my meditation cushion
is like an information booth at Grand Central Station,
and I am the small boy who wanders over
and says, "I've lost myself. I don't know where
to go." And the nice lady says, "Just wait here.
Someone will show up." And someone does.

Early Foundations

INTIMATIONS

I can recall in sixth grade having the simple perception that the way we see and speak of things as separate isn't true. I perceived that reality was greater, more unified, than the discursive mind could manage or depict, and yet all of us were somehow content to miss the essence. That's how I might express it now. At the time, it was just a non-verbal knowing that all that we experienced was *one unspeakable thing.* I remember standing on a street corner with a friend who seemed quite sympathetic to what I called the car-truck-lamp-post-garbage-can-sky-cloud theory of existence—or the idea that we could never describe reality without simultaneously naming the entirety of every interconnected thing we could see or think of all at once. So we would play a game of trying to reel off every name, object, observation, and sensation that poured into the mind at once, as if it were one long word. Because our separate words divided what was, in fact, all one thing. And though we never got very far, we knew what we were trying to do and why.

At thirteen, I felt an almost painful need to know everything I could about Tibet. It might have just been the sense of mystery. I gazed at photos of the Potala (the palace of the Dalai Lama). Having read somewhere that there was a lake behind the Potala, I searched, to no avail, for a photo of the Potala from behind. (I never did see a representation of the lake until I saw Brad Pitt skating on it in the movie, *Seven Years in Tibet.*) Not long after, I saw an ad for the Rosicrucians in some Sunday newspaper. It depicted, as I image it now, someone lying against a stone slab with a beam of light radiating upward from (or downward to) his third eye. It had a lead caption that read, "Spend a Minute in Eternity." I was just a little atheist Jewish kid, now living on Long Island—but I looked at that beam of light and thought, "I want that."

At fourteen, I enrolled in a book club called the "Mystic Arts Book Society." (It was another ad I saw; and the publisher turned out to be not far from where we lived. I got my father to take me down there to enroll. The guy behind the desk looked up at my father, either quizzically or disapprovingly, and said, "You know, these books are not for kids." "I know," I piped up definitively.) My first selection was *Cosmic Consciousness* by R. M. Bucke.

Bucke was a nineteenth-century Canadian doctor who had had a spontaneous enlightenment experience. Wanting to better understand it, he combed through the canons of Western literature, ancient and modern, and the early translations from the East. He investigated the writings, as well as the available biographies, of mystics, poets, and others who seemed to describe such an experience, attempting to formulate the common criteria of the experience, as well as the common factors that seemed to promote it. And so I was steeped in these biographies. Bucke concluded that this "cosmic consciousness," as he came to call it, was an emerging faculty of consciousness in human evolution. He later befriended Walt Whitman. From Bucke's long personal association with Whitman, as well as from Whitman's writings, Bucke—from his mid-nineteenth-century vantage point—judged Whitman to be the most developed state of cosmic consciousness to date. Needless to say, Whitman was an early hero of mine.

The second selection to arrive (did I choose it, or did I fail to send back the refusal slip?) was a beautiful two-volume boxed hardcover set of the first publication of *The Hundred Thousand Songs of Milarepa*, the spontaneous teachings of the renowned Tibetan yogi-saint. (It probably cost what a paperback book costs now!) This publishing treasure, which I inspected with awe but couldn't fully appreciate at the time, still sits on my bookshelf today.

Aside from these outer memories, I have a firm recollection of my inner state. And that is because I consciously and deliberately "sent a message" to the future. Sitting in front of a window, somewhere in my fourteenth year, I was overcome with a deep sense of absolutely knowing something that I couldn't describe, and which maybe I wasn't supposed to know. I thought: "When I'm older, I'll have no idea what I already knew at fourteen." So for safekeeping, I deliberately planted this moment in my memory, and also sent it as a mental time capsule into my future. Somewhere in my late forties, I opened the capsule in the form of documenting it in this poem:

fourteen

when I was fourteen I sat by
the bedroom window in the late afternoon
and looked out through the storm and screen
over a lawn and a suburban street and the
houses and the sun not quite setting through the
telephone wires and saw the great haze of the smog
settling over the world and suffused with a light
and a voice that spoke of a secret behind
all places and all times

and that voice moved like a wave
over the curve of the heavens and entered my
window and trembled in my body saying
I am here I am you You know what I am
and in that moment I knew that I knew what
needed to be known for all my life.

My oldest son recently shared with me a very comparable experience he had gazing out of a car window at the age of thirteen. I have since seen similar references in other autobiographies. There is definitely some faculty of knowing that calls at us; and I believe we are developmentally equipped to begin picking it up by early adolescence—if it is not drowned out.

Another significant experience occurred when I was fifteen. I had pulled a paperback book off my father's book shelf called *The Universe and Dr. Einstein,* which was a popularized treatment of Einstein's theories. I took the book along with me when my family left that summer for a two-week camping trip around New England. I had been immersed in the book on the afternoon we took a break from camping and paused at a lodge that had cabins and an actual dining room. The family was getting ready to go over for dinner, and I was sitting at the kitchen table locked in consternation over Einstein's idea that time was relative, and that someone speeding across the universe in a spaceship would be in a totally different time frame than someone on Earth, and would age more slowly. I was struggling with the conventional (Newtonian) view that time and space are absolute and equal everywhere. I could not fit Einstein's relativistic teaching into my own mind frame, and yet I accepted that it was widely understood as the scientific truth. So I tried to stretch my mind, and bang my head against it, so to speak—but my mind simply could not accommodate it. It was, perhaps, my mind's first *koan*—"the mosquito biting on the iron bull," as they say. Suddenly, my mental stubbornness gave way, and I saw that my grasp of reality was governed arbitrarily by the structures of my mind—and that when I let go of those structures, reality was open-ended. Rather than trying to fit a new reality into an old structure, I realized that the structures themselves could release, and reality was simply what it was, not beholden to my mind. And my mind soared free to embrace the new understanding. It was a sudden realization, a eureka moment, and it happened "just in time," under the pressure of my parents saying, "Come on already. We have to get over for dinner."

To this day, over a half-century later, I recognize the gift of that one moment—that freeing up from Aristotelian logic—every time I am exposed to the deep paradoxes of truth, and to the inexhaustible non-exclusiveness referred to in the next chapter. I now see that this greasing of the mind—a fundamental willingness to release its structures, and my discovery of the joy of that experience—would serve me in all future growth. Certain non-dual concepts that the discursive mind would ordinarily get stuck on were spontaneously cut through like butter—even at the conceptual level—owing to that original restructuring or de-structuring of my approach to reality.

By sixteen I was getting exhilarating and humorous premonitions of a reality that was vast, spontaneous, and free, just beyond and within the conventional way we structured our world. These premonitions spoke to me as adolescent epiphanies as I walked down my sheltered suburban street. This budding faith and delight and sense of intuitive knowing was confirmed for me when I opened my first book on Zen (Suzuki's *Essays in Zen Buddhism*), fortuitously handed to me by a high school teacher. Reading for the first time something that I privately sensed, I started calling myself a Zen Buddhist. At the same time, I found myself puzzling over why periods of happiness came and went. Why, when I seemed to establish myself in well-being or happiness, did this state inevitably turn into periods of distress or unhappiness—even if not much had changed outwardly? And why did life always come full circle to be a worrisome problem again? The same seemed to be true for everyone else. It almost seemed like a law of nature. Why should that be? It seemed to have something to do with the mind. I remember walking down that same suburban street formulating my "theory of the impossibility of continuous happiness." It said, basically: "Our happiness seems to be dependent on positive images and perceptions in the mind, which are impossible to sustain. Furthermore, because the mind is based on the recognition of opposites, even if a positive perception registers consciously in the mind, its negative polarity—the possibility of its opposite—registers unconsciously at the same time; and that unconscious negative identification will arise like a seed planted in the mind that must inevitably sprout." That was my first attempt to wrestle with the mechanics of the mind.

Two years later, in a period of crisis, I would have occasion to come face-to-face with the real work of Zen. And a year after that I discovered that there were actually teachers available in America.

GOD?

Meanwhile, despite my mystical inclinations and attractions, even to the Christian mystics, I had never crystallized my own clear, subjective sense of a personal relationship to anything like "God." It was something my humanist upbringing had not necessitated. Having been raised with no religious structure, either positive or negative, "God" was an emotionally neutral word for me—though I had largely dismissed belief in God as superstition. Now, as I followed my own intellectual thread, I was brought to that door; and it would gently, and somewhat matter-of-factly, open.

At seventeen, while studying Joseph Campbell and comparative mythology at Goddard College, I stumbled upon a long paper by Heinrich Zimmer on Indian Tantric Buddhism. I recall the potent phrase that stood out for me while reading: All the gods are in us. By the end of that paper, I had realized, or concluded, that we all occupied the psycho-spiritual space of the Infinite, at whatever level we chose to relate to it or name it. And that the Infinite was, in fact, *both* our infinite capacity for relationship *and* the widest canvas for our relating. It suddenly seemed obvious that this living and conscious Infinite was our foundation, and that we were not only in relationship to it, but that it was also *inherently relational,* none other than the fullest dimension of our own truest being.

A truth so basic needed its own big but simple name to represent it. And, well, "God" was as serviceable a name as anything for this infinite relational reality. Now, with no resistance, the word was free to assume for me a numinous character.

From that point on I was comfortable with, and equally drawn to, both God-centered and non-God-centered ways of talking about an all-embracing reality, and comfortable with both personal and non-personal ways of experiencing my engagement with It. I felt that *both* was more complete than *either*. (Generally speaking, I would regard "both-and" as more reliable than "either-or" when it comes to anything, from the most mundane truth to the most abstract ideas. I recall once saying to a friend that I thought "and" was the second-holiest word in the language. "What is the holiest word in the language?" he asked. "Yes," I said.)

IDENTITY VS. PRESENCE

Ever indulgent of my romantic and anti-intellectual side, and having already left school once to hitchhike across the country and work in several places as a farm and ranch hand, I now decided to fulfill my dream of shipping out on a freighter. The American Merchant Marine, and its union, was out of reach for me. But I learned that if one hung out in Brooklyn in the halls of the Norwegian shipping companies, every so often a position arose that needed to be filled. That fall semester I informed my college mates of exactly what I planned to do and announced that I wouldn't be showing up for spring semester. That winter of 1964 I put my name in at the Norwegian Union Hall and hung out in the streets outside the hall, talking with others who had scored such work from time to time. Along with encouraging advice, I also received various cautionary tales about what it might mean to be a small eighteen-year-old, and lowest in the pecking order, in the hold of a Norwegian freighter. By February, my name was called and a job was actually offered to me. I was poised to fulfill my latest dream. And then: the cautionary tales came flooding in and played havoc with my mind. When the final moment came for me to accept the job, I refused it. That is: I chickened out.

I was a failure and a disgrace to myself. I had invested my winter and, more importantly, had invested in a certain image of myself; and I had left myself high and dry. Worse than a person without a life, I was a person without a self. I was at the start of a full-blown identity crisis.

I ended up returning to school that spring with my tail between my legs. More than embarrassed, I was nurturing a private despair. Any coherent sense of self that had developed over my lifetime felt like it had been wiped away. I felt like I had, in one false move, stepped off the relatively reassuring escalator of my life and identity into an endless void, a hell-like tragedy from which I would never recover, wandering eyeless in Gaza, bewailing the taken-for-granted promise of my youth. At the very least, I would have to learn to live all over again.

All of that drama, of course, was a testament to the power of the mind, and the power of identity. But that last sentence—about having to learn to live over again—was quite true.

I did have one asset that did not abandon me: a commitment to the truth. Miraculously, it had fallen overboard with me. That capacity was able to observe and make note of what it saw. I observed a pathetic figure who outwardly carried on in school in a seemingly normal way, but who inwardly was flailing to get an identity back. I saw my ego constantly sorting through a ticker tape of possible roles, meanings, conclusions, identities, ritualizations, appearances, justifications, and strategies in the course of needing to establish and believe in a renewed identity for myself, one that was somehow logically consistent with what had been before. I could hear the variations on a constant mantra going through my mind: oh, maybe *that's* how it is; or maybe *that's* who I am; or maybe *that's* what will work. I saw that the principle of identity was king, and, in its absence, the ego's first job was to get it back—even if it had only random bits of papier-mâché to work with. Most of all, I saw, in the midst of my everyday life, that everything I thought, said, or did had one of two ultimate purposes: to look better to myself, or to look better to others. And I knew it was a sham.

(Of course, the task of a healthy ego, as it outgrows its adolescent or midlife identity crises, is to achieve a mature integration that is broadly congruent with the reality of one's life, and hence stable and flexible, not so self-involved—even open and magnanimous. But even that adult ideal is a vulnerable construction except to the extent that one has incorporated or surrendered to the *underlying essence* beyond identity—expressed as a fundamental capacity for pure *presence*. But now, in my adolescent crisis, I beheld the delicate machinery of that whole construction.)

One morning, early in the semester, I stumbled into the college bookstore, and my eyes came upon a book that I venerate to this day as one of my root teachers. It was *The Supreme Doctrine: Psychological Studies in Zen Thought,* by the French psychiatrist and student of Zen, Hubert Benoit. Though at times a bit abstract or metaphysical in its presentation, it was ultimately, for the most part, the most exact and practical technical map of the mind and the ego that I could have asked for.

Benoit laid out in penetrating and painstaking detail all the mechanisms of ego I had come to recognize, made clear why they were all based on a false premise, and explained what the true inner work consisted of. I lived with that book as my guru for the rest of the semester, literally reading a paragraph or two at a time, and not continuing until I had applied what I read. I began developing a clarity and a faith about a principle of being that was deeper than the principle of ego— one that, for me, really kicked butt. Today I would simply describe that principle as *attentive presence;* such humble and gentle words, but the fiercest of warriors. Attentive presence was a sword cutting through all my ego attachments and images. It gave me the courage to relax and disidentify from any of my beliefs or needs regarding the past or the future—and from any of the arguments, promises, or fears of the ego. Courage is needed to face down the identity and survival beliefs of the mind; courage not to grasp or to push away. Courage not to *not* feel, but to stay present for feelings and not identify with the ego's judgments or solutions for them. And I saw that *presence* was the gateway to a self more uncontrived and fundamental than anything the ego could come up with.

As I recalled all of this in the course of this current writing, I sensed there was another principle that revealed itself to me at that time—one that was a companion to presence. But it was eluding me. As I remembered and felt back into what I was experiencing and how I acted, it finally came to me: *sobriety.* I think of sobriety as surrendering the allure of, or the addiction to, a change of state—or the ego's attachment to "feeling better" as an end in itself, such that it rules our emotions, behavior, or clarity of mind. In my case, I recall not indulging in "relative solutions" for feeling better, nor permitting myself any giddiness or attachment to those things that affirmed me or made me feel better. I just toed the line.

Though all my deepest experiences were still far away—and life would always present me with the normal run of pleasure and pain, trial and error, and success and failure—the principle of presence always held firm. And though life would always give occasion for self-correction, life's corrections never became occasion for either fundamental attachment to, or doubt of, who I was. Looking back at my life, there was no greater single watershed moment than this. Between my "identity" and the "simple truth," I realized that the simple truth was holding me, and was the better bet.

One year later, I learned that there actually were Zen teachers available in New York City. I immediately began studying with Yasutani Roshi in New York in 1966, and began a lifetime dedication to meditation practice.

GOD, GUILT, AND HOMEWORK

In the mid-fall of 1965, after working some months as a farmhand in Oregon, I hitched down the coast of California to meet up with friends in San Francisco. In Sausalito, I was introduced to an unusual young man who invited me to join his friends overnight and share LSD on a beautiful cove north of Marin. LSD was not yet illegal, and they were quite seasoned—whereas it was my introduction.

We dropped acid in the early evening, and I began my classic journey through heaven and hell. At one point, as the awe of the experience was building, I actually had the conviction of standing at God's feet. God was an immensity of conscious being rising before me up beyond the sky and filling the universe. And yes, it *was* as if God was sitting on an immense throne, and I could barely see past his ankles. (So I couldn't tell if he had a white beard.) But he had condescended to give me a remote wink.

Heaven was the beauty of the universe that opened up all around me, and was in the depth and dimension of it all. Hell was nowhere around, but was entirely in the trip my ego came to lay on itself. Heaven—the seeing of our true nature—is, as in the death experience, gifted first. Eventually the ego catches up and pulls us away according to its tendencies. Ironically, I was not in recoil from the light, as such. But I was fixated on the profound guilt and shame that I didn't know how to die, how to let go of a separate self. And it was that *guilt* that sustained the ego's separation; its fixation on itself. Essentially, that was the recoil.

It seemed apparent to me that I was meant to surrender, or die in some way, into all this Oneness I was experiencing; but I was painfully aware of an ego that just didn't know how to do it. It was visibly evident to me that I and the ocean and the universe were all one thing. And I longed to walk into the ocean and just keep walking. Fortunately, a very functional ego kept me from doing that. And yet, in that state of mind, I managed to turn that healthy choice into an inadequacy! In my unprepared state, I did not know how to appreciate, or navigate, or relax with the difference between relative and absolute truths; it seemed like all or nothing, with no middle way. Simple attentive presence didn't follow me here. I had not as yet had any meditation training, which would have made all the difference.

After a long period of outer awe and subsequent inner pain, I went unconscious and slept the rest of the night on the beach. I came back to consciousness lying on my back in the morning, with the sun already upon me. I felt very peaceful as I lay there with my eyes closed. Suddenly I became aware of someone stroking my arm very lovingly. I had never before felt such a palpably loving touch. I thought of the people I was with and tried to imagine who it was that could be expressing so much love. It seemed amazing to me that anyone could convey such a profound radiance of love through their touch. It poured through my body and filled me with delight. After soaking it in for a minute, I finally opened my eyes with anticipation, and saw a fly walking up and down along my arm.

I returned to school that winter with two primary takeaways from the whole experience. First, of course, with the recognition that God and the universe truly were infinite and beautiful. And secondly, I also recognized that the universe had no interest in laying a guilt trip on me—but that I had homework to do. There were ancient traditions that had a proper understanding of these things—of the ego's relationship to the infinite—and I would just have to study them. So it was with a therapeutic urgency that I returned to Goddard and spent the semester steeped in Indian (Hindu) spirituality, thought, and civilization. Zen practice would commence that spring. It would be my only acid trip.

LIBERATION?

My studies at Goddard continued with a focus on Eastern thought, and its approach to reality, human potential, and liberation. Then, turning back to the West, I tried to understand what the Western equivalent—or contrast—was with regard to the full liberation of human potential. Where did the mutual potential lie for individual realization and humanity's realization? How was its subterranean call finding its way through the Hebrew prophetic, Greek philosophical, and Romantic poetic traditions? Or through Marx and Freud, and through industrial and post-industrial society? What was the actual biological, instinctual, and spiritual construction of a human being and his relationship to his world? What part did the East identify, what part the West? Where was the biological meeting point of Freud and yoga, the dialectical meeting point of Marx and Chuang-tse? What was the way out of a growing one-dimensional and essentially totalitarian hold over our politics, our economics, our consciousness, and our imperial domination of the Earth?

At twenty (1967-68), I wrote an undergraduate thesis at Goddard, contrasting what I called the "Eastern and Western dialectics of liberation," and also discussing the basis for a non-dualistic psychology. Then I gave up academics to study Zen and to work in Appalachia.

The next fifteen or so years of Zen, koan study, and other meditation practice allowed for a great emptying and clarifying of the mind and its dual structures, so that absorption in a state of lightness was easier to come by, producing a growing transparency between myself and reality. But it was a bit like plunging into the ocean with a light bodysuit on, seeing my oneness with all around, but knowing I still wore a membrane of separation. This was a miss—and a mile—from a direct awakening experience, when the bodysuit not only dissolves but "has never been there." It was only in my mid-thirties, while engaged in other practices, that I began being offered that naked level of direct experience.

Jacob Boehme

1575–1624

What had begun as fluttering
within the flower

of a familiar morn, became
a shuddering in that miracle

hour; turning familiar
all that was ever born.

And looking up into the world
of light, he knelt down

on the carpet of the
grass; and that carpet was

no other than the
stars, which ringed the heavens,

and it was not night.

Inexhaustible
Non-exclusiveness

*I*n the mid-eighties, I attended an intensive retreat of the kind I referred to in my Introduction. It was one I had experienced before, and which I myself had been trained to facilitate. Termed "the Enlightenment Intensive," it combined contemplation of a basic koan—in this case, I was working on "What am I?"—with communication in a dyad.

In this process, we are seated across from one of our rotating partners for forty minutes at a time, alternately engaging in our own contemplation and communication process, or otherwise giving silent witness to our partner's work. A retreat such as this looks and sounds very different from a meditation retreat, as we are encouraged, within a structured and boundaried format, to communicate to our dyad partners what is arising in the mind (and then to let it go) as a result of our contemplation of self. (Our contemplation, of course, may actually be shallow at first—or nonexistent—but gradually deepens, especially as the mind is emptied out.) This communication is not intended to be an intellectual report, but a complete presentation in every way—emotionally, energetically, verbally—of what is most true in that moment of our experience of self. The integration of communication into the contemplative process, as practiced here, seems to foster disidentification from the contents of the mind, as well as a greater embodiment of non-conceptual insight and experience. Along the way, this can lead to moments of drama, as well as to profoundly intimate moments of sharing—and self-awakening.

As virtually all of our rising thoughts, images, and reactions are indirect experiences of ourselves that we are identifying with, the communicator is encouraged to neither inhibit nor identify with them, but to remain present, and to immediately inspect each experience and expression contemplatively with the inquiry *who is that?* or *what is that?* Normally we utilize every experience, and our reaction to it, as an occasion to add to our story, to "pad" our conscious or unconscious assumptions about who or what we are. The point of questioning—to become the *question* rather that the habitual answer—reverses this process by allowing each moment of experience to return us instead to simple openness, and to our intention to be available to deeper perception or understanding. This method can allow for a flowing, integrative, and profound contemplative process, and for profound moments of realization in which the entire content of our lives and consciousness may be seen into and through. Of course, participants will differ in their experience in, and capacity for, doing such a process accurately.

I had flown into Toronto for this retreat, to a community and a respected teacher that had been practicing together this way for some time. It was late summer amidst a northern heat wave. Day temperatures must have been in the nineties. We were in a rural retreat center that had cabins with bunk beds like a summer camp. At night, I lay in the upper bunk bed in an uninsulated cabin, staring at the ceiling a foot or two above my head, and it felt like one hundred degrees. In the morning, I was eager to get to work with the thirty or so other participants. Soon the morning echoed with the anger of a woman across the room who was furious at her boss and "happy to be away from the son of a bitch." And she let it rip. No inhibition there, and no apparent contemplation; just a lot to get off her chest. Fair enough. In the course of the day all the contents of participants' minds came pouring out.

This was an understandable and encouraged part of the process, though I was a bit surprised by how much sustained energy was going into the drama by some whom I had assumed to be more practiced in contemplation. By late in the day, not in an especially deep place myself,

I began to feel a growing consternation and irritation at the level of verbal distraction and weird obsession going on around me. Perhaps in coming here I had fantasized some image of a deeper level of experienced practitioners and contemplation that would help carry my own work along. And now, in a perfect egoic set up, I was swilling a mix of frustration, judgment, disappointment with my own mediocrity, and a confusion of unexpressed energies. My tried-and-true disgruntlement knew no release, as by the end of the day the same woman was yelling with the same unrelenting vituperation about what an asshole her boss was. *Where was I?* I wondered.

Well, the first day can be quite a rollercoaster, I reasoned. As I had experienced in the past, each new morning allowed for a new shift of energy. But the opening dyad of the next morning started right off with screaming about the boss from hell, as if no night had intervened at all. In retrospect, I am grateful for it all. As the second dyad began on Saturday morning, with the craziness piling up around me again, I found myself sitting across from an earnest fellow; and, on my turn, I began to communicate precisely what was arising for me. I described the ongoing tension that seemed to be creating a protective hide all around me. I described what seemed to be a subtle gesture in my whole being, which was not just physical, actively pushing back and wanting to shut off the world, as if there were a membrane that seemed to define my relationship to it all. And in that moment, I got it. I instantaneously got it. I instantaneously, non-conceptually, directly got it.

In that moment, I noticed and communicated the nature of my own inner activity. My whole self was about the gesture of shutting out the world. And I simply stopped. I can't describe how I stopped. I didn't do anything to stop. The recognition and the communication and the stopping came together as one event. I simply stopped. The membrane of self vanished and the world came flooding in. And what came flooding in was love; for that was absolutely all there was. All arising phenomena, the screaming and the yelling, the air and the cushions, the inside and the outside of all experience, was love. In fact, none of these truly existed at all, or as anything other than the love that was simply the only reality. Every individual in the room, and every way that they were expressing and manifesting, was love manifesting precisely as them (i.e., precisely as love) in this moment.

It was not the mind's anemic or hopeful observation or conclusion that there was love underneath all this, or that we should recognize the love that really is inside people or that is seeking to be expressed through them. There was no *inside,* and there was no *through.* There was only the absolute reality of love itself. Every molecule of every being, every vibration or sound, was only the ringing substance and expression of love. Nothing outwardly changed. The same people were carrying on in the same way. The same woman was screaming about her boss. But it was all an ambrosial symphony of love delighting the ears and delighting the soul, which was itself nothing other than the same love. Nor was it just that I felt loving. Rather, everything was manifest as love.

The experience continued to grow and open in its revelation, and I continued to communicate to my partner as it was happening. I began to describe eyes of infinite compassion looking out through my eyes. And then I suddenly experienced looking out through the eyes of Jesus on the cross. I seemingly *was* Jesus in that moment. And I could speak for him with authority. I saw clearly what he saw as he looked down at the agitated mob yelling and hurling insults, totally lost to themselves. And I saw that what he said was not: "Forgive them, father, for they know not what they do." What he said was: "Father forgive them, for they know not *who they are.*" They did not know that they themselves were love and could only be love. So they were acting out an apparent drama of un-love. That is all we ever do. But it doesn't change all we ever are.

This primary reality of love, as it filters or is refracted through the mental structures of duality and the mechanisms of the ego, is what appears as the full span of our normal human relativistic sentiments of love—those that may often turn into their opposite—as well as our deeper capacities for compassionate action, or for that rare faithfulness to a deeper principle of love even in the face of apparent negativity.

But now, this love was revealed as the emptying out of all relativistic structures—mind and matter, time and space; it was revealed as the empty infinite self-originating and self-ecstatic holographic nature of being. My awareness opened into a reality that cannot be defined by mind or awareness as we ordinarily experience them. And here is where I will try to be innocently precise with words about that which one cannot put into words, and which contradicts the mind's dualistic logic.

Conventional structures of mind empty to reveal what neither exists nor fails to exist. That which never comes into being and which always *is*. That which is always an infinite potential, and which is always spontaneously realized. That which is no thing, but which is each thing. It is exactly a non-temporal, non-spatial potential of infinite probabilities without "self." "Without self" means without an abiding or self-existing reality other than a playful potential—and which is yet a wholeness of being, our infinite mind or infinite love.

It is not as if this is something known *by* the mind in a discursive sense. It was something I was directly seeing or understanding; the mind is co-equal with the understanding. This is to re-experience that the awake nature of the universe—experiencing itself as what it is—is not other than what we experience as mind itself. But it is mind divested of many layers of projected and self-involved reality that characterize the conventional world of our experience. It is one Mind (or Self) realizing itself at various dimensions of its flowering out from the heart of its own reality.

That flowering includes the flowering of non-dual into dual; the flowering of a timeless and spaceless dimension of inclusive potential into all the possibilities of time and space, personal and impersonal, one and many. It is hard for our minds not to think temporally or spatially— that all this happened *at some point,* or *somewhere,* as if first there were timelessness, then it manifested as time. But there is no before or after. This is now the very moment in which all potential inheres as one reality; and no potential—realized or unrealized—is exclusive of any other, as we are also not exclusive of each other.

This is the ever-present matrix of all realities, flowering out of an interpenetrating reality that is inherently friendly with itself as its own body, at home equally and simultaneously as existence and non-existence, participating in the same totality. It is like seeing into the heart of a holographic image, into the underlying structure and dynamic of the hologram itself. It manifests as anything, yet that "anything" is but a reflection of the reality that contains the whole. This is thus the ultimate divine intimacy, in which love is simultaneously total *and* transactional. That is, love not only *exists* as love, but *loves* as love, a Self-manifesting intimacy of "self" and "other."

I realize that this description is almost too dense to pack into words. That is perhaps why mythology—or art—exists: we need story images we can relate to. (It is what I have spoken of elsewhere as the infinite poetic nature of reality, because it is a non-literal reality that is the creator of all poetries.) But here's an image for you:

Imagine a big circus tent in which all the performers are part of the same healthy family, and are actually a playful reflection of the same performer. They share the unique family intimacy, love, sense of humor, and confidence of children who know they can go off into the world and become anything they want, without ever leaving the intimacy of home. They know they can be welcomed back at any time with great laughing cheer by their brothers and sisters—who are all the same being anyway, taking turns playing as them. They are absolutely secure in both their diversity and their intimacy, and hence the very reflection of "healthy parenting." Isn't this the very model of healthy relationships that our own soul longs for, lost as we are in a world of separate and reified images, guilt and blame, and cause and effect, in which neither diversity nor intimacy are secure? It is the healthy parenting offered by our true nature. It is the generous non-exclusiveness that is all-creating, all-supporting, all-forgiving, and is love everywhere. It is our deepest archetype, against which all else is unconsciously measured.

We use myth because all rational concepts fail to apply here; we are no longer experiencing at the level of mind at which concepts either operate or are relevant. Hence, all words or concepts, however inspired or precise, mislead. In contrast, the awake absence of concepts leaves us transparent to this inclusive reality.

Yet, all words, all beauty, all love, all personal-ness, all life, are also a perfect expression of this reality. That is why my realization so naturally proceeded—centrifugally, as it were—from the initial fact of letting go of all resistance to this present human reality; to melting into the ecstatic, visceral, wet, everywhere observable reality of all-pervading love as the only thing that exists; to the experience of universal compassion through the eyes of Jesus; to the interpenetrating heart of infinite, all-inclusive, timeless-spaceless reality which is not other than what this is now.

The words that arose in my mind and which I believe I said out loud were: "inexhaustible non-exclusiveness." Inadvertently, this constituted as much of a verbal answer as I had to my original question: "What am I?" By *inexhaustible* I meant to convey that one could never come to the end of—never arrive at any exception to, and never limit the eternal abundance of—the generousness and full extent to which nothing was in any way other than, or exclusive of, anything else; a conception contrary to the conventional tendency of all our seeing. Everything *includes* everything else. And this is the very body of love.

I lingered on my cushion long after all others had left for breakfast—with the exception of one of the retreat staff, who remained sitting against a far wall. I looked at this woman, whom I had barely noticed before. I was aware of all my capacity for not noticing, and all my routine unconscious ways of reinforcing the shell of my false separateness—that very same constrictive gesture that eventually exploded in my realization. Now she was the immediate *other,* the one whom I could continually choose—consciously or unconsciously—to include in (or exclude from) the open field of relational reality. I remember looking up and simply saying to her, "I will never exclude you again." And though I meant it in a tearful and heartfelt way—a kind of cosmic confessional and a repentance—the poor woman couldn't have known at that point what I was talking about. Such explanations would have to come later.

It is, in fact, the full relational field in which we exist together with all things that is the consummate flowering of this non-dual reality. The awakening to other underlying dimensions (or contexts) of perception is an occasion for integrating the roots of our awareness in the indigenous ground of our own being. Yet this perfectly manifests in our interdependent life with others. It is to imbibe a little more of the underlying spaciousness of phenomena, non-fixed, non-literal, non-self-centered— so that we may more readily open up space where conventional experience might close space down. And it is to take mature responsibility for the affirmation and renewal of inter-relational life together, amidst the challenges of finite experience that trigger our conviction of separation and negativity.

The profound glow of this experience faded—much to my surprise—as I reentered into the hard work of the Intensive, though its openness rebounded after it was over. However, it was in the months that followed that I realized how authentically something had entered and shifted in my body. In fact, it was *the world* that had entered my body, and in some new way I had entered the world. I experienced increasingly that my body was the body of the world; that somehow I had entered into the evolutionary journey of all life with a kind of bodily compassion; that the non-exclusiveness was an instructive and constructive bodily event.

There is an integrative sense of this in the physical body itself, but the bodily event is actually larger than the physical: it is the body of our identity with all things, spontaneous and beyond concept. If I am not distracted from this truth by a delusive mental preoccupation, then being at rest in my body is being at rest in the body of all around me. This cup, for example, inhabits me, and I inhabit this cup. You inhabit me and I inhabit you. This is not physical. It is the body of reality. But it registers as a seemingly physical experience—because my own body, or bodymind, participates in this experience.

After this when I did any physical healing work, I felt a complete continuity or extension between my own body and the body of the person I was tending. The same was true if I was sitting with someone on the emotional level. But "extension" implies a spatial extension that is not accurate. It is more a mutual inhabiting. Or, as Whitman says in "Song of Myself," "every atom belonging to me as good belongs to you." The bones of the world are my bones, and I feel it in my bones. At the same time, as I have said, there is a natural oneness with, and commitment to, the entire body of our evolutionary journey as human beings. I would characterize this body of universal identity as "the body of compassion." It is only in my later years that I have been graced with experiencing it equally as "the body of gratitude."

Perhaps you may recognize any of this as something you have experienced or intuited at one time or another. This is only natural. For these experiences are what underlie our everyday experience and may assert themselves at any time. In truth, this awareness is always present in a usually unrecognized form. We overlook our own awakeness simply by not allowing it space to declare itself more fully, distracted as we are by our habitual ways of knowing and classifying experience, and of moving on to the next thought or belief. Hence, there needs to be an alchemical process of cooking—a process of intention, intimacy, and surrender—by which the obstacles to seeing and recognizing may be clarified out over a lifetime.

The nameless and unknowable reality out of which all else manifests is the *Ein Sof* of the Kabbalah, the dharmadhatu of Buddhism, the tao without a name birthing the tao with a name. And we could speak of this dynamic in a very impersonal or philosophical, or even scientific manner—as the "mechanism" of creation or of reality. Buddhism has been seen in this impersonal way if we overlooked its glowing and ecstatic heart. But "impersonal-ness" would mentally flatten the experience. There is no need to reduce our deepest experiences of personhood from the fullness of our Buddha-nature to some purely impersonal detachment. Or to "science's" arbitrary and unscientific invalidation of subjective consciousness. Our personhood expresses as our ability to feel the bubbling spring of consciousness, to laugh and to enjoy; as our commitment to take care of the world around us, and to experience the grief and praise of eternal transitory reality. It is even our willing embrace, in love, of those learning experiences that "crucify" our perceived separateness.

For at the heart of this experience—at the heart of reality—is an awake presence, an infinite intelligence. At the heart of this reality is a deliciousness of being that we might call personhood, though not in the separated or fictitious way we usually think of. This personhood is the body of reality and is innately relational with itself. This personhood is equally present and not present, because it is not separate from experience. This personhood is equally empty and full. It is simply a name for the way the universe is awake and alive to its own existence at all levels of manifestation. It is the moment of recognition between us. It is the clap of thunder over the mountains. It is the blossoming and fading of spring, or the slap of the Zen master's hand. It is accidentally dumping your ice cream on the sidewalk and laughing.

All is the universe giving birth to itself. That unceasing and eternal birth is the timeless and spaceless generosity, or generativity, of inexhaustible non-exclusiveness expressing as us. When we awake as that—when it takes birth in us—it is, as the Tibetan teachers express it, the Original Mother Light of Being awakening in us as the Child Light, which recognizes its Mother and is one with Her.

The profound Christian mystic Meister Eckhart so succinctly captures, in Christian language, the essence and the import of this eternal birthing: "Here in time we make holiday because the eternal birth which God the Father bore and bears unceasingly in eternity is now born in time, in human nature. Saint Augustine says this birth is always happening. But if it happens not in me, what does it profit me? What matters is that it shall happen in me."

And that is the only place it is ever happening.

It's That Simple

It is because I saw
the jeweled net of non-exclusiveness—
the infinite impossibility
that something could be other than anything else—

that my body became intimate
with its own world;

that my cells suffered the ultimate vulnerability
of being not other than you
in an imaginary
extension of time and space,

and that I am forever in your debt,
which is my joy,

and will not deny you;

and why tenderness gathers like dew
in the fold of a leaf
and catches every sparkle
of sun, every nuance of rainbow,
sky merging in sky.

It is because I awakened
as the jeweled net of non-exclusiveness,
the inexhaustible love that merely is
the within and the whole
of all things,

song within song,

and that our bodies are wrung out of such delight,
that my heart could not exclude you,
and that my body

includes the deliciousness of your form,
the ecstasy of your formlessness,
the irresistible celebration
and support for your every aspiration;

that I can pledge myself to you
and never leave you,
but lo, I am with you always,
even unto the end of the world.

It's that simple.

The District of Lu

*A*bout a half year after this experience, I was conducting one of my evening groups in which we use the dyad process. I was also participating, and working on our familiar koan: *Who am I?* It happened to be my birthday. My partner had just begun the process by giving me the instruction, "Tell me who you are." I quickly experienced what felt like falling into an infinite center. My being seemed to be falling forward, and as it fell it became emptier and emptier, until it was nothing at all. And yet, at the same time this was happening, I found myself deliberately saying, "I am Paul Weiss, I am forty years old today, I have a little red VW Rabbit, and I drive eight miles to work." Sounds ordinary. But it was a direct perception of the identity of the relative and the absolute.

There was no question that saying, "I drive eight miles to work" was any different than saying "infinite emptiness." Or that saying "I am Paul Weiss" was any different than saying "no one at all." They were non-exclusive. "Eight miles to work" *is* infinite emptiness. So is every idea that has gone into constructing Paul Weiss, who is still Paul Weiss driving eight miles to work. I later recalled the story in which Zen master Joshu responds this way to a question on the nature of reality: "When I lived in the district of Lu, I had a coat that weighed three chin." He might have said, "I had a little VW Rabbit and drove eight miles to work."

It is natural for the mind to take any word—whether it points to the absolute or to the relative; whether it says God, basic space, dharmadhatu, or original emptiness; or whether it says Paul Weiss, drive to work, little red Rabbit, or happy/sad—and make it solid, and to make a distinction by the very nature of concepts. But if the conceptual realm has been erased, the "unity" or the "distinction" of dharmadhatu and little red Rabbit are both laughable. There is even no subtle hierarchy or causality, as when the mind says: "Yes, they are one; infinite emptiness is *arising* as form." No, sorry. There is *no arising*. There is *no taking form*. There is *no sequence*. There is *no relative or absolute*. There is *no identity*. We are simply That. It is freedom.

There are certain koans in Zen, my teacher once explained to me, that are considered wiping koans. That is, they just serve as a little tissue to wipe away any snot left over from the last experience. This little experience felt like that in relation to the previous experience described. It wiped away any snot of subtle difference.

0

What things are
cannot fit into a thought.

The road crew reluctantly
puts down the picks and shovels,
and goes home.

The moon has yet to appear
over the crumbling asphalt.

Last night three crows
flew past the moon.

But they are gone.

The Pterodactyl

EMOTIONAL INTEGRATION

In the early nineties, I began a few years of intensive therapeutic emotional work (and subsequent training) in a process that was both meditative and expressive, and which facilitated a simple regression through many layers of my emotional substrates. What this kind of therapeutic journey and regressive work shares in common with all meditative or contemplative work is a conscious and willing suspension of left-brain activity and ego-organization to allow the intuitive and holistic perceptual field of the right brain to function freely and consciously. The right brain is not only capable of resting in the holistic present, but is also capable of accessing the sensations, wisdom, and, we might say, cellular memory of the body. The cellular wisdom of the body, in turn, has access to still wider fields of information that the left brain knows nothing about. Consciously exploring, in a therapeutic container, with permission to give bodily and emotional expression to all the dimensions of my thoughts and feelings, beyond all ego defenses—and regressing back to infancy (and beyond)—was unimaginably liberating and integrating. It left me in compassionate friendship with even the "darkest" parts of myself; and hence, also more capable of comfortably and empathetically accompanying the depths of my clients' journeys, wherever they needed to go.

There is a great misunderstanding of the nature and potential of this regressive work, both in the therapeutic and, especially, in some spiritual communities. There is a critique of emotionally expressive, or cathartic, work in certain circles—certainly in Buddhist circles—with the legitimate concern that these processes (including primal therapy, expressive anger work, and others) merely use emotion to re-stimulate and reify old emotional story lines and drama, rather than contributing to new levels of mindfulness in the present. And it is true that some expounders and participants of this work may get attached to the idea of the emotion or the catharsis itself as the ultimate liberation. But this is not so. The real point is our awakened listening, not the dramas or the stories themselves. Still, the bodily and vocal expression of emotion may be, in fact, a most important part of the healing process. Why is that?

When we are mindful of emotion in the present as a chemical tide of feeling in the body, we can allow it to be instantly "self-liberating," by bringing an integrative awareness to the emotion that is neither suppressive nor reifying. Then it is allowed to resolve its course as a cycling of the underlying life energy. But we have each accumulated a lifetime of emotional history in which no such integrative or liberating awareness was present, and which is now held in our implicit memory and cellular function. That is to say, it is a deep part of our identity. These emotional substrates are bodily energies that never had the chance to be emoted or expressed from the body, nor empathetically recognized and integrated.

This unexpressed and suppressed emotional history that still lives in all of us contributes to what is sometimes referred to as the "inner child"—an aspect of us that has not been free to mature into the living present because of a complex of unconscious identification and unexpressed and unresolved experience and emotion. It maintains a holding pattern that our mature awareness must learn to recognize, listen to, and attend to. A large part of the resolution of a child's distress is in being heard. And it is our own mature awareness that must do the work of hearing. One level of empathetic hearing is to re-allow the child's feelings into our mature awareness. A still deeper level of empathetic listening may come from "hearing" and allowing the child's reality to fully and bodily express the feeling. A greater depth of freedom and of insight may come from the bodily and vocal enactment, as the "child" is more fully received into the present. For many, this has been found to be equally true for the repository of pre-born experiences.

The body itself is a repository of emotional wisdom and the wisdom of healing. And this work actually requires a deep contemplative listening as we surrender ourselves to the body's wisdom. The insight and the integration this work allowed me was as significant for my life as any "mystical" revelation vouchsafed me. Entering into the body to liberate or integrate our emotional truth is not unlike the *bodhisattva* entering into hell to save all sentient beings. It makes us more fearless and more truly available to others. The point, again, is not the old stories or emotions, but the awakened and compassionate listening that allows them to be reintegrated and released in the mature present.

I am inclined to distinguish that which is sometimes referred to therapeutically as the "inner child" as, rather, the "inner child complex." That is, it is actually a complex story line that has captured and suppressed our true inner child, and which is still held in the body as a living part of us. And yet that *storied* inner child must still be loved back into the fullness of our being. Our *true* inner child is true of us right now. It is the Christ Child, so to speak (if I may use that archetype), of divine innocence and openness that we were and are. That Christ Child is ever born into the world with absolute vulnerability. And, in our ultimate human development, that Christ Child will flourish and mature into a Christ Adult. But the vulnerability of the child subjects it to the wounds of its dualistic experience that it does not yet have the developmental maturity to resolve (and which distorts its continued mature development).

Ideally, it is the adult who holds the protective container of awareness and empathy that carries the integrative function for the immature child. This requires the genuine developmental and empathetic maturity of the parent. And it equally requires a true reciprocity of communication and emotional reality between child and adult, such that the child's reality feels fully received, held, acknowledged, and resolved. This resolution occurs insofar as the child has learned that her emotional experience occurs within a field of genuine connection to, and reciprocity with, others—rather than requiring a separation or protection from others that would lead to forming a separative and fixed internal reality.

Obviously, the former often fails to happen; recognition, and reciprocity of communication, is not adequately established. Adults themselves become the source of the child's distress rather than the container for their healing. Hence, true communication—true listening—plays a sacred role in liberating fixation and in welcoming us always back into the genuine and living field of mutuality and relationship—which is the essence of the dharmadhatu itself. Similarly, the mature work of all human beings is to welcome back and make whole, in the midst of our own experience of fragmentation, the wholeness of our original inner child, so that it may complete its mature integration as our divine adult—open to the complete dimension of *what we are*. Thus it is not the emotion, the catharsis, or the dramatic reenactment itself that is the liberating factor, although the energetic release may offer a significant cleansing and healing of the body from stuck emotional energy. Rather, this emotional expression must occur in conjunction with a deepening of our present integrative consciousness that is able to welcome the movement of feeling back into our total being.

CHOOSING DUALITY

The processes of emotional integration that I have spoken of here are not in themselves the central subject of this book; yet they are of equal stature. And in my high regard for this kind of work, they feel like an essential dimension of the story. Our emotional healing is central to evolving and integrating the breadth and depth of our capacity for genuine reciprocity, compassion, attunement, and empathy for both ourselves and others. And it is often bypassed in our "spiritual" preoccupations.

Furthermore, this emotional integration process depends on the conjunction of cellular wisdom, intuitive right-brain listening, compassion, receptivity to subtle fields of information coming from both within and without, a suspension of fixation, and an innocent nonconceptual dedication to the truth. These all play a part not only in our mature and integrated emotional and psychological development, but also in our human capacity for revelation beyond the structures of our thought. In that regard they are all a part of the human mandala of both healing and wisdom. And they are all relevant to the process that leads to the following experience, which I would not be quick to label either spiritual or emotional, nor a *satori* experience, but which was nevertheless surprising, revelatory, and instructive.˙

This was not an occasion when I was processing information and feelings that took me back through this life, nor into the womb, nor into conception, nor into past lives—all of which I have experienced to some extent. No, I wish to speak of an experience of surrendered regression that seemed to portray my "soul's" first entrance into this "earth world." By soul, I mean one of the infinite holographic projections of Original Self that is expressed as an "individual." The soul-self reflects the light of the Original Self just as sunlight is reflected and dispersed through so many raindrops—not dualistically separated in nature from its source-self, and yet individuated in its expression. The raindrop refracts and disperses the full quality of the sunlight, just as the soul participates in the full quality and experience of the divine Self.

It was as just such an individuated divine self that I entered the earth plane; that is, our current common plane of discourse. Please understand that all of this language, and even all of our visionary or regressive experience, is necessarily metaphor. "Soul" is just a word for our essential nature. "Earth plane" is just a name for a realm of experience. Presumably metaphorical as well was the very clear vision and experience of my first conscious incarnation on the Earth as a pterodactyl!

(Please don't get lost here either in literalism or in scoffing disbelief. I don't know if I was a pterodactyl. This was simply the mind's form, I presume, in which the subjective experience came to me. And for me it still has a certain poetic truth.)

I experienced myself embodied as a primitive flying creature—my mind experienced it as a pterodactyl—in a much earlier geologic age. In my regression, I suddenly was aware of flying above the Earth of an earlier biological landscape. And though I was seemingly incarnated in this pterodactyl form, my awareness was still co-equal with my non-dual divine nature and with the universe. I was still divine equanimity, awareness, and bliss; not separated from, or forgetful of, my wholeness of being. Not other than God. I was simply assuming this form and, with great pleasure, flying in the earth sky—which was also the divine. All being was still inherently fulfilled and complete in its true nature (as in essence this world is).

Then I saw—I remember the moment critically—a shadow move across the Earth below, which I thought of as a small mammal. At this perception, in a sudden unexplainable moment, there arose in me the all-consuming desire—call it lust, call it hunger—to capture, to eat, to consume that small mammal. It was, at that moment, the only compelling reality. It was the very birth of hunger. In that critical mysterious existential moment there was a seeming choice away from the unified peace and wholeness of my experience, and toward a fundamental duality—a separate self-awareness all consumed with the object of my desire.

It is fascinating to contemplate now this simultaneous arising of desire and dual consciousness. It seemed like it was that spontaneous instance of desire that itself triggered my choice to forego my divine awareness in favor of the dualistic consciousness of an obsessively grasping being. Yet, what inherent (creative?) potential for duality allowed me to succumb to a desire for something more partial than my actual being? What allows us to say: I can either have bliss or I can have "that"—and we choose "that"!? Is that not the very story of our lives? In any case, that moment of desire—I remember veering off course to give chase, to pursue—was the true moment of my entry (my "fall") into the world, and the birth of my individual karma, my individual identity, on the earth plane. It was a complete transition of consciousness.

I suppose all that could be depressing. But the experience was revelatory and exhilarating, as visions tend to be. It opened a vastness of perspective, and yet brought my attention back to this moment. I saw the mechanism of our choosing duality, of the willing surrender of our God-nature, that is every moment true of us. That primal drama is occurring with each recurrent opportunity to choose our separateness over our inherent wholeness, and to choose our craving over our inherent satisfaction or completeness.

This is the natural drama of biological life that must feed on life, but the drama is all the more reified and fixated within the evolving cognitive capacity and ego consciousness of our human species. For us, every act seems to set forth an echo of emotion, imagery, and projection that structures and solidifies the story line of our virtual world. It contributes to the complex structure of "self" that is not easily released. Hence, we do not simply feed. We also create an imaginative world and history of separation—of greed, anger, and ignorance—that is culturally and psychologically institutionalized. Thus, the moment of clarity and choice—our own creative complicity, moment-to-moment, in the world we are experiencing—is lost to our awareness and understanding.

Until we recognize this, and turn our awareness back on our own process, the knot of our fictive reality gets drawn ever tighter. On this the many wisdom teachings will lovingly counsel us, each in their own way.

Good News

disregarding dreams,
transparency is working
even when we're thick.

this is like sunlight
filtering through a lead room
as if it were glass.

then only the lead
believes in its heaviness
while the worlds rejoice.

it displays the bright
reality of spaciousness
in which it rests,

creating its dreams
of lead in a river of
shining emptiness

no wonder the sun
shines anyway, the grass is green.
it has always been

transparently the
same. That day we are awake
to our beginning.

A Feather on
the Breath of God

*J*esus made it very clear, echoing all wisdom teaching, that our own
chronic judgment and blame both creates and sustains our own subconscious conviction of sin. It is both the fiber and the glue that jails us
in our separate-self story. Forgiveness is the get-out-of-jail-free card. In
the Aramaic language, the image conjured is of holding on to the end
of a rope that ties ourself and others to a virtual past by maintaining a
blame story. Forgiveness is the reset that allows us to start fresh with
the grace of the present moment, that allows life and spirit to unfold,
that allows God. It is a blessing we can offer others and ourselves. Thus,
the same shift that enables us to truly forgive the trespasses of others
allows us to find our own trespasses forgiven.

A Course in Miracles gives a very succinct explanation of this dynamic.
Our subjective sense of a separateness from God, or from Reality—and
of further defending and promoting a separative self-story—is accom-
panied by a conscious or unconscious sense of guilt that is projected as
a conscious or unconscious conviction of God's—or Reality's—anger
with *us*. This is further projected back by our own chronic anger at, or
blaming of, Reality (or God)—in whatever form. The two-edged sword
of this guilt-blame-shame cycle, which helps to lock the ego into place,
is of course reflected in our guilt, shame, and anger-based political and
religious dogmas and institutions. This, on both social and personal
levels, is precisely what Jesus came to liberate us from.

The English anchorite Julian of Norwich, in *Revelations of Divine*

Love, gives an account of her mystical experience in which, coming into the presence of Jesus with her fully inherited and culturally reinforced conviction of sin, she is amazed and disarmed to experience that the whole drama of sin is unreal and insubstantial, and that Jesus is only the face of love.

So we can never, in reality, be in retreat from "God's anger and judgment," because God has no anger or judgment. We can only be in retreat from God's love, or from the boundless generosity of the dharmadhatu. And the dynamics of that retreat are compelled by our addiction to, and defense of, the false structures of the self that cannot be sustained, but only become obsolete, in that love.

This became clear at the very start of another Enlightenment Intensive that I attended in the early nineties. It was the very first dyad of the very first day. I must have entered the dyad with a critical self-awareness, even grief, over my inadequacies, or my failure to live up to my aspirations to love. As that was what was present, I started right off with my litanies of confession and repentance.

But as I was earnestly accounting each sin, or failure to love, the whole affair quickly became transparent. I was empty space in a sea of empty space. And some great power of consciousness and love was shining through me as if it found no obstruction there at all, but only empty space. "God" was not looking at my "sins," which were only my projected shadow. That power could hardly be concerned with such a paltry and imaginary construct. My sins are only the structure and the glue of my own self-story. I found myself lifted in that transparency, as weightless and sinless as a feather lifted on the breath of God. I was no more substantial than that. I had no separate substance by which I could cast a shadow. No personal future; no story, good or bad. How presumptuous those stories are.

As creations of light, we are always seeking light. The light is the truth of us. But conventionally, we seek the light as extensions of our own story in our own projected worlds. As we are loyal to these worlds, we turn from the light itself, and from its potential to "destroy" our life.

But as we open, the light only outshines our fictions—that is, anything that is not light itself. And our true lives are lived as extension of that light. Nothing we care about has died, but only offered back to us in the light of love.

Re-reading this, I could see this book perceived as a giant mixed metaphor. Are we light? Or are we infinite emptiness? Or are we "a little teapot?" Or are we inexhaustible non-exclusiveness? Yes; in the absence of literalism or dogma, there are only mixed metaphors!

the ecstasy of table manners

sitting at your table
where everything is you

you teach the secret etiquette
of the meal—

eternity in the lift of the spoon,
devotion in the pouring of tea,

where ecstasy of the whole
is the intimacy of every act,

the love feast is in the incidentals,
and every incidental a portal

into the mind of the Host—
that's how you have caught me

my hands in my lap
gazing into a bowl of cream

On the Subway

AWAKE, EMPTY, AND INTIMATE

The paradox of non-dual teachings is that the world of non-duality is not other than the world of duality, and vice versa. Otherwise, "non-duality" would be dualistic. Duality, with all its implications, is only a mode of perception, natural to our minds, and is a natural potential of non-dual creative consciousness itself. To further the paradox, when we perceive only duality, we fail to see into the true nature of duality. Whereas, when we perceive non-duality, duality shines in all of its fullness. The non-dual nature of reality, so counterintuitive to our discriminating consciousness, can only be made evident by an immediate shift in consciousness, and can only be described in paradoxical or metaphorical ways. Then we are able to perceive that *this right now* is an inexhaustible non-exclusiveness, or the *completeness* that our dualistic perception instinctively seeks but fails to grasp.

That dimension of inexhaustible non-exclusiveness is referred to in some schools of Buddhism as the interpenetrating totality and potential of the dharmadhatu, the fundamental space of being that is *undefined presence* itself, *empty awareness* itself, and *creative responsiveness* itself. Out of this fundamental space all arises, and, despite appearances, we are never other than this. We embody within ourselves the vast playful potential of the dharmadhatu—the inconceivable Ein Sof of the Kabbalah—which includes the paradox of our fundamental *wholeness,* our perceived *separateness,* and the *dialogue* between those two aspects of our being. It is a poetic dialogue, as it arises not out of the fancied literalness of our discursive minds, but out of the creative poetry of a playground of paradoxical and infinite relationship. Every poetry captures another dimension of that play. This poetry includes the genuine poetic contributions of each of our known systems and languages of spiritual insight, depiction, and understanding. And each of these spiritual poetries reflects the truth—when they are not suffocated by their own dogmatic literalism.

It is the psychological and spiritual genius of Buddhism to recognize and express these abstract ideas as the immediate reality and potential of consciousness. That *present aware being* that is the nature of reality is *our* present aware being. It is even the essence of our discriminating minds. *Rigpa* is the Tibetan term for present aware being that is immediately available to us when we are undistracted by the reification of the mind's content. Yet all arising (and distracting) thought and appearance is also recognized as the radiant energy (or *tsal*) of aware being itself (*rigpa-tsal*). That is to say, therefore, that awareness and all the arising objects of awareness are one. They share the same intimate truth of being that we speak of abstractly as the nature of reality.

But, of course, this intimacy of experience, the intimacy of the knower and the known, is sundered by our mind's habitual perspective. Buddhist psychology (and Freud would agree) would point to the mind principle (*manas*) arising within universal awareness, reflecting back on a limited and fixated field of awareness, and identifying with it as a separate self; identifying the rest of the field as a separate external world. And, by extension, the "self" *identifies* with, and clings to, its various ideas, attachments, and projections in lieu of recognizing *essential awareness* itself. The *empty intimacy of awareness,* and the inherent *intimacy* of self and other, is replaced with, and distracted by, our *identification* with the content of our thoughts and projections.

I have come to think of *identification* and *intimacy* as the two contrasting principles of consciousness. Because all of our mind's content—including the idea "me"—arises *to* awareness, awareness is not ultimately the possession or the property of an individual self; rather, it is the fundamental and universal creator or principle in which all arises, including the idea of "separate self." *Identification* is the universal consciousness imagining and identifying with an idea of itself that is less than—more partial than—its actual being (as my "pterodactyl" did); and projecting a world based on that identification. We do this routinely. Although it is a contradiction in terms, we might say this is rigpa getting lost in the rigpa-tsal. Some Eastern traditions characterize this as God getting lost in God's own creation.

Intimacy is the natural state that exists in the absence of that fixation, identification, and projection, when the inherent oneness of conscious being is simply open and manifest to itself. And, even within the play of relative forms, you and I are able to be present to each other in the same way, as an expression of our inherent intimacy, not as a defended idea of separateness. In the realm of human psychology, ego is a naturally arising function. Still, we tend to consider the "healthiest" ego to be one that is not fixated on its separate identity to the point that such identity excludes the possibility of intimacy.

When awareness rests in itself, and is not identified with its separative imagery, nor distracted by the entirety of its own content, it is experienced as awake, empty, unbounded, non-self-centered, and intimately available. We may even have an occasional and unnoticed taste of this in our own brief, relaxed moments of simple awareness. All appearances ultimately abide in this real, or relaxed, condition of existence itself. This real condition, the inherent intimacy of being—the inexhaustible non-exclusiveness—that underlies all of our mind's projections and separations, is the Buddhist dharmata, or dharmadhatu; the fundamental space of being. If we speak theologically of "God" as the fundamental space of being, it might even be called the actual *Mind of God,* prior to separative mind. (Or, as the Indian saint Kirpal Singh once put it: "God plus the mind equals Man. Man minus the mind equals God.")

VAST OPENNESS

Within the playground of our spiritual experience, there appear to be many complementary modes of experiencing essential truth. Some of these modes may be described as more *introverted* experiences: some variation of "seeing through" the projections of outer physical appearance as only a screen for the underlying truth that is of the nature, or structure, of consciousness itself. The other mode is a more *extroverted* seeing, and a welcoming of all outer appearance as already not other than the warm and transparent manifestation of truth. My own experiences reflect both. The two modes are not exclusive of each other. Both are present together, for, after all, they are one and the same. They are double reflections in the same glass; but subjectively there is a shift in emphasis or recognition.

It is a thrilling testimony that the same infinitely creative truth will forever be experienced by us humans in infinite flavors, colors, perspectives, dimensions, subtleties, and varieties of love play. And that is because God is a lover. Even the same experience is never the same twice. Every poem is a new poem. In a previous book I spoke of an experience in 1994 that arose while riding the New York subway. It opened onto the same vista as my earlier experience of inexhaustible non-exclusiveness, or of the primordial hologram of being. And yet it was different in tone, in blessing, and in its facet of realization. And that is always so. When you enter the mansion through so many different doors, you get different views of the room. Perhaps in these two instances the difference reflected one experience arising from an intensive, searching practice, and the other arising spontaneously from relaxed openness. I don't know.

I described it previously, in my book *Moonlight Leaning Against an Old Rail Fence,* as follows: "As I sat on the subway heading downtown, resting peacefully at heart and open to the buzz of subway activity around me, the scene melted—or should I say, "*being* melted"—into what I never find better words for than "the great transparency." It was like entering a mirror in which all the objects are arising with limpid clarity, and yet with no substance of their own—"being and non-being, form and emptiness, simply transparent to Itself as one and the same, resting in one awareness. Any linguistic description can't help but imply a subtle distinction that is simply not so. Form *is* emptiness. Emptiness is *exactly* form." I remember feeling, "This is the mind of God."

The poet Robert Bly has a playful phrase in one of his earliest poems, "Shack Poem," that says, "how marvelous to be a thought entirely surrounded by brains!" And I felt as if I was experiencing everything as insubstantial, and as intimately at rest and at home, as God's thought would rest in God's own brain.

My earlier experience of inexhaustible non-exclusiveness was like a bird's eye view of the whole manifesting structure and dynamic of creation. But what distinguished this experience was the fully embodied, extroverted luxury of looking around at length and perceiving all this creation *from within* as a vast openness, an eternal and immaculate purity, still, and undivided by being or non-being. There was no sense of "seeing through," but rather that it was all already "shown through." And it was the luxury of sitting on the subway as if it were the jeweled pavilion of eternal being spreading in all directions, even as I casually witnessed the immaculate emptiness of all beings and all arisings. Person by person. Sign by sign. And that in the midst of all this limiting drama of birth and death, there was actually nothing subject to birth and death. It was vast emptiness always and already at rest in "God's mind."

"There is nothing that can be known that isn't exactly this," I wrote immediately after. "Past and future, time and space, aging and death, the subway, the city, all desire: a dream within a dream, as we sit here with compassionate indifference to that which has never been and will never die."*

---

*See Paul Weiss, *Moonlight Leaning Against an Old Rail Fence* (Berkeley, Ca.: North Atlantic Books, 2015), 37.

And there came with it the sense of infinite peace extending in all directions, and yet *sounding* with the choruses of a silent divine music, a thrill of holiness. Like "hosannas unto the highest," I wrote.

I was delighted to discover years later this quote from the ancient Japanese Zen master Keizan, which exactly echoed my experience: "There is not a speck of dust for ten thousand miles. Where are clever officials and fierce generals now? There is only singing, singing. All is Great Peace from the very beginning."

THE PARADOX OF SUFFERING

As I looked at each person on the train, I saw their eternal being beyond all worries of birth and death. The "indifference" referred to above was the clear awareness that everything is *already taken care of.* So in that moment there was no drama, no storyline of despair, nothing needing to be done. And that peace carried with me onto the city streets. But if that is so, if all is peace and perfection, where does suffering, and where does compassion, come in? Transcendent realizations aside, the relative reality of suffering—the universal subjective experience of suffering wherever it is experienced, and whatever its foundation—is not meant to be airbrushed out of the picture. We know it well from all sides. Rather, it awakens in our awareness our intrinsic maternal compassion, which supports all beings, and which is the function of God's own compassion. The clearer the seeing, the clearer the compassion.

Did those same human beings resting in God's peace not also betray their own discomfort, their lines of worry, their distractions, their unknowing hurtling under the city streets through the vistas of their own needs, avoidances, hopes, and fears? Did they not, in their own small way, reflect the wider canvas of suffering on this planet? The absolute and relative truths are not separate domains. They are interpenetrating aspects of one reality. God is intimately and compassionately aware of the suffering of his own creation. Our divine emptiness, sometimes blissfully revealed, is equally our empathetic recognition, our dedication to, and our compassion for, all beings. The Buddha-mind and the Buddha-activity exist only as a function of that compassion. To "have no compassion due to a nihilistic conception of emptiness," the Tibetan master Longchenpa tells us, is "an error in perspective" that is "like a dark abyss."*

There is obviously a profound paradox here, one of the great mysteries of the creation: the essential Wholeness of Being, by whatever name you want to give it, manifests the whole creation out of its own love, holds it in its love, and, we might say, ministers to it and redeems it in its own love. This essential understanding is Buddhist as well as Christian, though the language may be very different. And to me this is not blithe theology. It is my own experience. It was also the experience of Julian of Norwich, when she wrote in *Revelations of Divine Love,* "God maketh it, God loveth it, God keepeth it."

On the subway, I saw that God—that is, an encompassing and sustaining Conscious Loving Presence—was keeping it all. And yet, between the holding and the redeeming, the loving and the keeping, there arises the profound experience of suffering, and the behaviors that contribute to suffering.

It would thus be easy for us to jump to, and reify, the idea of a self-originating evil that works against "God's love" or Buddhism's "basic goodness." Alternatively, we may allow for a more nuanced understanding of the *evolutionary* dimension of the divine process, which is simply this: as the non-dual reality of Creative Love and Awareness lovingly expresses itself as dual, it subjects a dimension of its awareness to the relativistic feedback loops of dual perception, limited perspective, and misconstruing of its own ultimate reality. This enables the false sense of a separate self, along with the delusions that Buddhism characterizes as the three poisons of greed, anger, and ignorance, to perpetuate a compound dynamic of falsehood and suffering.

---

*See Longchenpa, *You Are the Eyes of the World* (Ithaca, Ny.: Snow Lion Publications, 2000), 51.

There is also, however, an ever-present awake, or redeeming, dimension of God's wholeness, or of Buddha-activity, active in the creation—which is also the existential heart of our own awakening process. We *are* that, after all. Yet, from our human angle of experience, we find ourselves stretched between the realities of our profound capacity for compassionate and sacrificial love, and the profound pain and grief of a suffering world of which we ourselves are both enablers and victims.

Perhaps the passion of this existential drama is most associated in the West with the sacred heart of Jesus, which evokes both the infinite capacity of love and the profound sacrifice and pain such love must endure along its evolutionary journey in this world. For when, as I wrote above, "Creative Love and Awareness lovingly expresses itself as dual, subjecting its own love and awareness to the mirror of duality," this dynamic is the very archetype of all stories of "sacrificial divine passion"—of that Reality of Love that is three in one. It is, in other words, the abiding and infinite ground of love (the father); the finite expression in which that love experiences the relative consciousness and suffering of its own misconstrued duality and must evolve in awareness (the son); and the *dynamic* love that enables, reawakens, and restores (the holy spirit). Not as some drama of the past, or that happens over time, but as the integral truth of *this moment.*

Reflected in the story, imagery, and person of Christ and his passion, this dynamic is itself the "father-ground" of Being entering into the "begotten-ness" of creation—only to go through the trials, or evolutionary processes, necessary to redeem, or fully manifest, the inherent wholeness of our own being. When Jesus speaks of being perfect, he is not speaking moralistically, but of "perfect" in the sense that a whole circle is a perfect circle. I hear Jesus saying, "Be ye whole even as the underlying truth of you is whole." No one arrives at wholeness without the embrace of this paradox of love and suffering.

To my mind, the image of the cross represents the wide sacrificial embrace of this paradox—and its resurrection in truth. It also reminds us that at the mid-point of our own heart is the capacity for such embrace. The mature spiritual path calls us to do just that even in our everyday lives: not to dramatize in our familiar ways a childish reaction to the perceived absences of love, but to exercise our agency as the redeeming source of love's activity and choices. This is the "Christ-path" that walks the road between the diversions of a false materialism on the one side and a false spirituality on the other. To the extent we are able to walk such a path, it might be said to be only with the help of the "holy spirit," and, yes, *wakan tanka,* the active dimension of awake presence and evolutionary support in the creation.

This also accords with the Jewish passion of *tikkun olam,* our shared commitment with God "to heal the world," to re-knit original wholeness through the quality of our attentive presence to all things. And, for all its reputation for a dispassionate equanimity, Buddhism also shares this Christian passion. It recognizes the same paradox of wholeness, love, suffering, and liberating activity. There is no more passionate or elaborate invocation of the path of sacrificial and redeeming love than in the Mahayana literature of the bodhisattva path. As with the holy spirit, there is no less in Buddhism the redeeming principle of *bodhicitta*—understood as an individual moral commitment to awakening and to service—which also came to be understood as the essential activity of love and awakening within reality itself, the Buddhist *paraclete,* the active principle of redemptive wholeness.

Listen to these eighth-century words of Shantideva in *The Way of the Bodhisattva:* "For as long as space endures, and for as long as living beings remain, until then may I too abide to dispel the misery of the world. For those who yearn for land, may I be an island; for those who seek light, a lamp. May I be a protector to those without protection, a leader for those who journey; a boat, a bridge, a passage for those desiring the further shore. May the pain of every living creature be completely cleared away. May I be the doctor and the medicine; the nurse for all sick beings in the world until everyone is healed; a guard for all those who are protectorless, a guide for those who journey on the road. For those who wish to go across the water, may I be a boat, a raft, a bridge. For those who need rest, may I be a bed. And for those who need a servant, a slave."

Rumi speaks of "this love which is built of our desire for emptiness . . . " and says elsewhere, "Emptiness is what your soul really wants." But emptiness is not a realm. It is not a principle or a thing or an accomplishment or a separate reality. It is the space in which love flourishes. It is the space out of which love creates the world. It is our space right now. It is the New York City subway.

Unwrinkled

The world unwrinkles just the way it wrinkles.
The mind which wrinkled from space,
defining its own existence,
unwrinkles co-equal with space again. Images
float like milkweed in an air
where they cannot stick. My children
are talking of snowboarding. I've
been snowboarding all morning, enjoying
the snowy slopes of no more time,
the laughing hologram of never have been.

Dancing
at a Festival

Some of the experiences I record here were major, dramatic, or defining shifts of experience. Some, like the next, arose quietly and smoothly as just an ordinary moment of revelation, as natural as the next breath. Just an occasional moment in which reality pats us on the head and says, "Good dog."

I am sharing the driving with my daughter as we head north to visit friends in Montreal. On this occasion, my daughter is at the wheel, and I am in the passenger seat. It is an ordinary car moment: chatting of this and that, sharing our love for Leonard Cohen, joking, gazing at the roadway. I can't remember the exact details of the moment. But at some point, I have the memory of looking downward—to the dashboard, to the glove box, to the floor itself? Or maybe the vagueness of the vision stays in my mind because something was flooding into awareness more essential than the external visual screen.

I find myself suddenly gazing into the "river of being"—all existence just that. It is as if I am gazing into my own face in the river, but the face that is gazing back is "all-inclusive being itself." Here, in the car, eyes cast down—or somewhat down—I am totally aware of where I am, but gazing eye-to-eye with the hologram of being itself: a river whose only dimension is totality, and yet, "personally" gazing back as me and, like a mirror, showing all things looking out *from* me.

In a poem subsequently written about this occasion, I wrote: "When I first saw my face reflected in that river, I saw all things looking out

from that one face. And I saw that the river had never left its source."*
This captured the essential points: I, a shimmer of the river-of-all-being,
saw the river-of-all-being reflected back. I was not just an individual
self. I was everything else. And that river—dynamic and creative by
nature—has never left its source. That river, however dynamic and
abundant with the life of the whole, has never left home! It is ever the
abiding source also expressing as *active river*, with absolutely no separation. And it is our own intimate reflection, our own true face. We have
never left home! "We are all comrades, then," I wrote, "on a hillside in
spring; dancing at a festival from which no one has ever been excluded;
and no one has ever left."

What a balm to our long-searching hearts, to our wandering bereft
in the desert of our perceived exile. The daily reflections of the world,
and of our participation in it, all contribute to a reflected image of a
separated self, which screens our perception of existence. But when the
mental structures of separate self suddenly relax—for whatever reason—
when we see into that non-dual mirror, there is no separate self seeing
its reflection. There is only reality reflecting back its own wholeness,
shaking hands with itself, experiencing from either side of the mirror,
with all the warmth of a personal-ness that is not personal, the generous
fulfillment of its own being. We are that.

---

*See my book *Moonlight Leaning Against an Old Rail Fence*, 212.

Spring Morning

Dampness rises from the morning earth.
Smoke from the fire.
The body growls a bit and sends out its warmth too.
Rain in the air. The trees know everything.
Thoughts, feelings: it's all snow melt.
This growling is a subterranean hum. Let's growl along.
Something complete is moving as the earth moves.
Resting on our foundation, the universe is accomplished.
Heart recognizing heart. The rest is artifact.
Didn't we pass this way a million years from now?
I'm gonna let this timeless buggy take us home;
stick with what's true; sing with the clacking wheels.
Simple opportunity is given every day—
which we cast out with the morning sink water.
Trying to manage the world by thought is
like trying to balance a cup atop a gushing fountain;
or to operate the sunrise from a smartphone.
I think I'll let the day play me for a fool.
Be just as stupid as this rainfall.
Give me a ring, and we'll walk together.

Neither Life nor Death

*T*his next "ordinary moment" of revelation is one that I found, and continue to find, supremely instructive and serviceable. For it addressed—or should I say "undressed"—the key existential issue of our lives: life and death. It undressed, with a gentle yank of the robe, those reified categories by which we define—and confine—so much of our lives. It left in their place the simple affirmation of this "un-reified" moment of being—which is not other than our capacity to love.

I don't remember much of the sequence of this experience. I don't think there was much. I was home alone in the evening. I may have been meditating, or reading, or lying quietly on a couch downstairs, just before bed. I do have a vague recollection that, whereas in my previous experience I was looking downward, here I was looking upward, toward the ceiling. And I think I was just coming out of a now lost experience in which I had just had an image and insight about "inverted chalices." Something like the body and the universe as one chalice inverted on top of the other. As I recall, it was a pretty rich vision, but I'm afraid that's all that remains.

I don't know what triggered, in the next moment, the complete emptying out of life and death. But it was as if the air cleared of both, and I was left with a lucid, spacious, and essential transparency of being, in which even such ideas as life and death were obviously just mere "ideas." As ideas, they were both fictitious. Bogeymen. Surely, it must seem foolish of me to make such an outlandish proclamation. But they were clearly two paramount examples of how the structures of mind replace our direct moment of experience. For aside from the idea, or the labels, what we are experiencing right now is not life, nor death. What is real is no such "things," or categories, but only this moment of consciousness. Only this moment of conscious affirmation of being. Only the activity of our participation in existence, through our choice to be present (or, potentially, to recoil). And this is the expression of the loving awake presence that is the only reality. The rest, even "life" and "death," are shadow images.

What made this disclosure so serviceable was that it didn't lend itself to an *objective* knowing so much as to a clear *subjective* conviction about what is real and what is worth doing. It is love that is the only truth, and the only real meaning, to all that we call life or call death. It was as if the air had cleared for a million miles in all directions. Every limiting idea, every structure in the universe was a paper tiger. Empty. It fell before the lion's roar of love. It re-sprouted as love beneath our feet. There was only the freedom to walk on, loving with each step, and waking love out of the world.

By great serendipity, I happened to discover a few days ago a scrap of paper with the beginnings of a poem scrawled down on that occasion. It said, "All thoughts hang between the fallacy of life and death. Within this deep illusion, we choose the path that binds us to our fears." Another attempted line, and then I abruptly stopped and crossed it all out.

And then what came through instead was:

> *All of Life is false.*
> *All of Death is false.*
> *Love is true.*
> *Love beautifies life and death.*
> *Our attachment to life is only our resistance*
>   *to an imaginary death.*
> *Our attachment to death is only our resistance*
>   *to an imaginary life.*

Beyond life and death, love is
the lion's roar
and the silent bud.
There is neither everything nor nothing.
We are the big bang.

I later realized that this experience perfectly accorded with a long favorite aphorism of mine, which I keep as a primary mantra of remembrance: "Persist as love despite all evidence to the contrary." The world as we experience it—our *history* as we experience it—consists largely of the sum total of evidence to the contrary. It gives us every "reasonable" reason to conclude that "there is no love here," or, "I am not love," or, "I am not capable of loving," or, "such and such is not deserving of love." Such is the history of life and death; and life and death, in all their shades, are very convincing ideas. But whenever flustered or discouraged about how to proceed, there is only one true way forward; and there is nothing handier, nor more strengthening, nor more clarifying than to remember it. Persist as love *despite* all evidence to the contrary. It's the only thing that's true. It's the only thing that's true of *you*.

Gandhi once said (and I know this from my son, Isaiah, who wrote a song about it), "History is the record of the interruptions in the steady flow of love." Whatever healthy foundation of genuine love each of us receives in this life, such love is never the basis for our egoic, or separative, self sense. Rather, it is the foundation for our essential trust and openness to being, and our capacity to love others. It is an expression of the complete and reciprocal reality that we are. Alternatively, all of our developmental experiences that constitute a "disruption in the steady flow of love" contribute to the specific structure of our egoic history and the shape of our self-story.

The same is true of our species' experience. A lot of genuine love has been transmitted in our human experience, but none of it is the subject of, or the basis for, history. "History" is about the "accomplishments" of our separative existence, or about the despoliation, oppression, deprivation, or death of that same separative existence. Love, in and of itself, does not contribute to "history." It is simply the radical function of our true and integrative being, complete in the timeless present. But the structures of "life" and "death" require a history—a story of what we are or what we might not be. We live amidst this provisional way of seeing the world. But it has only relative truth. It is an institutionalized projection, or framework, identified with at the most radical level—so who would dare to question it? It is fictitious. An interruption of our experience of the availability of love now.

Sitting in meditation earlier this morning, before I returned to typing up this piece, and wondering just how over the edge I sounded in saying these things, I opened a book at random and was greeted with this deliciously simple and affirming quote from Thich Nhat Hanh: "Being and non-being are ideas in our head, just as birth and death are ideas. They are not objective realities. And it is the ideas we have to transcend if we want to experience nirvana."

And what is nirvana? Nirvana is this moment of being when we are not defined by our ideas or mental structures. It is the freedom to be/not be. That is why one famous Zen text says, "the way of enlightenment is not difficult for those not trapped in their own stories." Being and non-being are our deepest story. Quite naturally. But they don't own us. We can let that story suppress our loving, or we can let our loving beautify that story. Each moment we are the big bang—the singularity of creation. The singularity of love. There is neither everything nor nothing. Just our love quietly flowering, or trumpeting, into the present moment. Persist!

Sign on the Door

Dear friends, I am in spiritual retreat.
Spring is my cabin.
The sky of stars is my lonely mountain.
The awakening of life is my meditation.
Light and dark, my meditation hall.
Your happiness is my devotion.
Negativity and doubt is the subject of my fast.
Simplicity and slowness is my meager meal.

The weather of my heart is the dharma.
The wind in the trees is its recitation.
Equalness, its hidden delight.
Following the course of a brook, my esoteric path.
Home leaving is home return.
Comings and goings are my mantra.
Morning, my mentor.
Sound is my source.

This thundering silence is for everyone.
This smile is for you.

Welcome.

In the Arc
of the Fountain

THE FOUNTAIN

If you have the good fortune to be sitting by a large public fountain (as I am right now), take some time to empty the mind and just watch the fountain. Relax into that contemplative emptiness in which your mind is not other than the fountain itself. Then its secrets will reveal themselves to you. Your awareness will not be screened by the mind's concepts of world, water, shape, solid reality, and all the accompanying associations. Rather, the mind will dissolve into the holistic display of joyous activity and empty space—the mindless paradox that something so inherently dynamic can be so empty of all concepts.

If you study the fountain, you notice that the same water is recirculating. The drops that fall become the pool from which the fountain sprays again. Each drop *becomes* the pool and finds its way into a new drop; but not the same drop. And not the same trajectory. The pattern of the spray, the pool, and the whole reality of the fountain has an element of chaos that is at the same time one with itself—one light, one consciousness.

Thus the fountain consciousness is also present as, and seeing through, each drop. If provisionally hypnotized by its own reflection as a mere drop, the "fountain mind" will know itself as separate, subject to "good" and "bad," and doomed to death. But when fountain consciousness is awake in the drop, it reflects only the life of the whole fountain.

It is "dancing at a festival from which no one has ever been excluded, and no one has ever left." When the fountain is *love* itself, the light reflected between the drop and the fountain is only love. It is the nature of the drop to cling to its own reflection; and it is also the ultimate nature of the drop to let that go and reflect the whole of the fountain, to slip into fountain consciousness again.

William Blake said in *The Marriage of Heaven and Hell:* "The cistern contains; the fountain overflows." I think he was talking about the nature of "God" (the fountain), and the nature of our minds (the cistern). The mind wants to contain and "own" everything. It even wants to own or contain "God." It contains them with its concepts. But the world it contains is only the virtual world of its own concepts.

The fountain cannot contain, nor can it be contained. It is a living process, without a reified self to contain or be contained. The appearance of a fountain as a "thing" is an illusion. It is only the dynamic energy of its generous all-inclusive activity. I might say that the universe, or "reality," is an infinitely recurring fractal of fountains, down to the life of our own bodies. It is empty and all-creative. What it creates is Itself. It is creative at all levels and *is* what it creates. Each drop that is "cast off" joyously is the life of the fountain itself. Everyone gets to dance; and everyone gets to *be* the dance. Reality is a fountain of light in which each drop both *reflects* and *is* the light. Yet, whether we call it "Reality" or "God" or "the Universe"—all are concepts.

Awareness Now is the empty body, and only truth, of all that we project as "God," "Universe," or "Reality." Spontaneous awakeness that has no "being," but *is being*. That we *are*. No reality, no God, no universe, no fountain. No self. And yet, the bird flies by the great oak to land in the maple tree. And children are laughing on swings—or huddled in detention camps. There is careless joy, and there is the experience of suffering. And our heart is moved by both. We *are* both.

IN THE ARC

In the mid-seventies—long story—I actually suspended my formal Zen training, not without much inner conflict, to follow a call I little understood: to become initiated by the Indian guru Sant Kirpal Singh, and to immerse myself in the *Sant Mat* tradition and the practice of *surat shabd yoga,* or the yoga of inner sound. This tradition distinguishes between the essential listening and essential witnessing aspects of the attention, and teaches the surrendering of both the inner seeing and the inner hearing back to their source in the divine. It also makes use of a mantra, an inner repetition of the names of the divine, as a practice of attunement and remembrance, similar to *zikr* in Sufism, or to the Prayer of the Heart.

Its meditation practice is entirely inward and non-physically focused, gazing with devotion into the heart of whatever is arising, gazing into the heart of gazing itself—"intently, minutely, penetratingly," in the spoken words of Kirpal Singh. And it is also a listening into the heart of listening, open to the inner divine sound or music. "With longing in the heart, with silence in the soul, and with no thought of this world or the next," he advises. In its essential formless simplicity, it has the ring of Zen. Yet in content, form, style, and metaphysics, the outer aspect of this God and Guru-centered devotional tradition was about as inimical to my Japanese Zen training as could be. And the shift of meditational focus from the *hara,* or lower abdomen, to the third eye did not come gracefully.

Though its essence is non-dual and transcultural, the outer language of *Sant Mat* is laden with dualistic cultural and metaphysical assumptions that I had to make peace with in my own way. At the same time, I personally came to find at its essence, and in the guru, a teaching of great authority; a most formless teaching of the pure focusing and loving surrender of the attention, at every level of inner and outer experience, to that which is ever beyond its own content. Its paradoxical entry and demands on my Buddhist practice fostered a cross-pollination of understanding and practice in my spiritual life that was ultimately deeply expansive and functional. Still, its presentation doesn't offer the more neutral and transparent teaching vehicle that I instinctively gravitate toward in my communication with others. So while I am sometimes more reticent to speak of it, it deeply informs my spiritual understanding and remains a most personal dimension of my innermost practice.

After many years, I found I had resolved this conflict of paths at the level of essence, and recognized that my path is neither one thing nor another, but is rather, in a sense, Me—that is, my own immediate and mysterious unfolding and surrender to *who I am* and *what this is.* And my understanding has been nourished by all the ways our many spiritual teachings address this. In this I am always buoyed by a classic Tibetan Buddhist teaching which says, "Look not to the words, but to the meaning of the words. And look not to the meaning, but to the essence of the meaning." So I am, in retrospect, extremely grateful for this profound and enriching cross-pollination of my spiritual life, and the new breadth and depth of dimension it made available.

After the passing of Kirpal, I chose to continue my practice at the feet of one of his principal successors, Sant Ajaib Singh, with whom I spent time both here and in India over the course of two decades. During the years with Ajaib, I was graced to experience spontaneous and treasured moments of loving surrender and personal intimacy in his private presence, and sometimes in small groups. Externally, the culture of practice was not always so inviting to me. And I was not an easy disciple, as the cultural context and dualistic language of some of the teachings was not always true to my own instincts. Yet its essence held me. And so I needed frequently to return to the essence, not the language. The guru's eyes told everything. And I returned to their essence in my meditation. In the increasingly larger crowds, I might also experience a focused devotion—or, quite often, dryness, distance, or doubt about the whole affair. What a final blessing, then, that my ultimate and transforming experience of communion with the guru was gifted on the final occasion of being in his physical company.

The last time I got to sit with Ajaib Ji was in the summer of 1996, a year before he died. We did not know it would be the last time he would return to be with us. Before a large gathering of devotees, under a large tent, his talk commented on one of his own composed devotional songs, or *bhajans,* in which (reminiscent of the psalms of David) he asks God to turn and study "the pages of my heart," to inspect if there is anything but love there. (The phrase "turn the pages of my heart" is still one that brings tears to my eyes.)

As my mind fell into rapt openness, gazing at him and listening to his words, I began to observe a phenomenon that I had read about in the literature but had never personally experienced before. As Ajaib Singh looked out at us, I witnessed his face changing into the full countenance of his guru, Kirpal Singh. It was one of those eye-blinking, head-shaking moments. Yet it was still clearly his—and my own—guru, Kirpal, sitting there. And a little while later, his face turned into that of his guru's guru, Sawan Singh. The three faces began to take turns appearing as the speaker on the dais, with mounting glee and a large smile in their eyes. These three began exchanging themselves more frequently, as if they were having a delightful joke of it, having fun with us and a great time of their own. I seem to recall at some point letting out a laugh of delight. (But I suspect it was inward.) At last, the transformations became as rapid, dynamic, and joyous as a fireworks display—a grand finale, perhaps. Which might have signaled that the "end" was near.

My whole being was slowly opening and dissolving in the delight of it all, and I was being carried into a reality prior to form. As outer form dissolved, I experienced myself as only a radiant drop of spray in the light of a radiant fountain of love that was the guru as "Supreme Guru," supreme Source. (I do not mean this merely as poetic imagery of devotion. It was an immediate shift in the reality of my direct experience.) And as outer form became transparent, I experienced that this relationship was really all that was happening in creation, or within all infinite space as I was now experiencing it. I was a radiant drop hovering and dancing the way mist hovers and dances around a fountain; a delight-fully equal part of a greater mist, and of the intimacy of a fountain and its mist. Each drop of that mist had a non-egoic personhood that was not other than the radiant life of the fountain itself. And yet there was at the same time a most profound mutual lover's gaze between myself and the fountain, which was my source and my lover. It was delightfully personal, except for the knowing of myself as only a reflection of the fountain's love.

Of course, I did not "literally" experience God or Guru as a "fountain"—as if everything was gushing out the top of his head. But the relationship of a drop dancing around the fountain was the essential soul experience. This might also call to mind the Christian or Muslim imagery of the angels dancing around the throne of God, reflecting His love. Or as a drop itself might experience a fountain as simply the greater truth of its own being, and the source, sustainer, and delight of its own existence. And I rested and danced in the spray of that all-creative, all-loving source as it exchanged with me—at the most fundamental level of being—a most personal laughing, reassuring, and all-loving gaze, which wore the "face" (or smiling essence) of my guru.

It is experiences like the one above—occurring within or with-out the pantheon of Buddhist or of any other imagery or mental structure—that have made it easy for me to cross-pollinate in myself the spiritual journey of humanity, to appreciate the poetry of the soul, and to discern the underlying truth in a playful, all-embracing, non-fundamentalist way.

The non-dual mystics within all the Abrahamic religions—Judaism, Christianity, and Islam—all have their own way of pointing to the non-dual paradox of the everything and the nothing. The Kabbalah speaks of the Ein Sof, the Infinite that is not subject to our ideas of being and non-being, just as Buddhism speaks of *prajnaparamita,* the wisdom that goes beyond all our categories. To say, as these mystics do, that God is one, or that God is All, or that there is no God but God and none other than God, is to say that God inhabits and is reflected in all of creation *as* His own Self. And to believe there can be any part of what we are, or what we think, or what this is, that is separate or other than that is only an illusion of the dualistic mind.

Equivalently, the Buddhist sage Longchenpa, using a different metaphysical poetry, speaks of the "basic space of existence," which is the only true and present reality behind all apparent differentiation. He says: "Since samsara and nirvana do not stray from the realm of basic space, they are merely natural expressions of emptiness that have no basis."* He cites an earlier tantric text which states, "All there is has me—universal creativity, pure and total presence—as its root. How things appear is my being. How things arise is my manifestation. [Sounds, words, capacities, awarenesses, bodies, environments, experiences, etc.] . . . are the primordial state of pure and total presence."†

As in Buddhism, the Kabbalah speaks of the *yesh* (the appearance) and the *ayin* (the essential emptiness). In the imagery of the great Jewish mystic Shneur Zalman, for example, a ray of sunlight looks like a separate thing when seen by itself; but when seen against the sun, it is "naught and complete nothingness, for it is absolutely nullified in relation to the body of the sphere of the sun which is the source of this light and radiance."‡ Mature mysticism is not an otherworldly philosophy, however—for the very nature of that non-dual nothingness is to celebrate itself as the everythingness of this world.

All of this is a parallel metaphor to my own experience of being the drop that has no true existence other than the fountain, but in which the intimate love that is the fountain is reflected and alive in me.

We may also appreciate, looking at so many of these experiences collectively, that the vantage points of spiritual experience are myriad and various within the complete hologram of truth. God, after all—the basic

*See Longchenpa, *A Treasure Trove of Scriptural Transmission* (Junction City, Ca.: Padma Publishing, 2001), 296.
†See Longchenpa, *You Are the Eyes of the World*, 32.
‡Cited in Jay Michaelson's *Everything Is God* (Boston, Ma. and London, Uk.: Trumpeter, 2009), 67.

space of existence—is in the "business" of experiencing every dimension of its own being from every possible vantage point—and through every possible poetry. That means that *we,* our consciousness, can potentially experience—as I was shown in these several experiences recorded in this book—from the vantage point of, for example:

- the interpenetrating wholeness of being;
- the emptiness of all being;
- that emptiness expressed as fullness—or as individuality;
- emptiness reflecting itself;
- individuality identified with its separateness or personhood;
- individuality celebrating its personhood;
- individuality opening to its personhood in relationship to a personal God;
- individuality dropping the cloak of its personhood, and reassuming, or resting in, "the body of Reality," or God;
- or, as we will soon see, of being the very Source—or God itself—as Creator, Lover, and Created, in whatever spiritual language we choose.

We do a disservice to ourselves, to God, and to each other when we congeal around one point of view in denial of the others. Or when we literalize any point of view, or the expression of it, to the point where it must be either right or wrong. Everything is true!

And We *are* That!

In the years following the passing of Ajaib Singh in 1997, I found myself increasingly returning much of my energy and attention to Buddhist sources and practice—to *Ch'an* (Chinese Zen), and particularly to the study of the Tibetan sage Longchenpa and the Tibetan *atiyoga,* or dzogchen lineage, that points to the "great completeness" of this moment of experience. And I felt no conflict. My inner guru draws me and holds me in the magnetic field of the Source. And I still feel the guidance and influence of the guru opening my way in dzogchen study and practice. Life is gracious. It is "the great perfection." The Master used to say, "Master is gentle, and will draw the disciple through his or her path of least resistance." And I can feel the invitation for the next level of surrender graciously awaiting me and drawing me in. There is an inner organ of listening and beholding, an attending upon the spirit, that is increasingly transporting, though still rudimentary in my experience. But the gesture of *availability*, the inner surrender of the listening and seeing faculties to their beloved, is for me an ever more magnetic attraction and experience of the soul's coming into coherence with its origins.

imagine beloved

imagine beloved
if there were no you

and my love was constrained
to offering itself

to the shapes
of my own mind

imagine if our feasting
and secret meetings

were proscribed by my rational skin
or material bones

or by parents somewhere
who knew more than we

imagine if the wind's howl
and the blowing snow

were not the love nest
of our melting sighs

imagine beloved
if i were not you

I and My Father
Are One

THE TIMELESS OCEAN

In June of 1999 I attended a ten-day Ch'an (Zen) meditation retreat with the Chinese Ch'an master Sheng Yen. I had sat with him on two previous occasions, in the early and later nineties. On these occasions my meditation practice was what the Chinese Ch'an tradition refers to as "silent illumination." *Illumination* refers to the function of awareness, like a lamp simply and impartially illuminating all that comes within its field. *Silent* refers to the silence of the discursive mind, which does not discriminate, categorize, reify, or project upon what is arising within the field. Of course, the activity of the mind may well arise in all these ways; but, rather than identifying with it, we learn to include the movement of the mind itself within the illuminating light of awareness. And over time is does become more still.

This is essential and wide open contemplative awareness with no preconceived idea and no separate object, but for the comprehensiveness of experience. Nor does it distinguish between the "inner" field of experience and the "outer" field of experience; between illuminating the subjective activity of the ego that I call me, and illuminating so-called objective experiences. This is a key point. In the absence of such mental discrimination, and as awareness rests in openness to the all-inclusive field of experience, the familiar categories by which the mind learns to divide awareness, such as inside/outside, self/other, and better/worse, also come to rest. Nor is it merely a passive stilling of the mind. For it entails an active interest, an opening to—a "listening into"—the nature of reality, while allowing all things to appear of themselves.

In my own experience, this sitting allows for a progressive widening of the field of unified awareness, and for a progressive relaxation of the mind's boundaries. This may arise first as a unified field of mind/body awareness, and proceed to a unified field of mind/body and environment, and of the inner environment (self) and the outer environment (other). All of which leads to the unification of all experience simply as "Being" itself; and then even to the disappearance of the mind's subtlest and persistent distinction of being and non-being.

As with all deep contemplation, there is a delicate partnership (until one is beyond both) between willfulness and surrender; between intention and openness. The willfulness lies in the inherent offering of oneself through heartfelt attention, which, in turn, allows for a dynamic of surrender that is mediated by that which is already *prior* to the self.

So although this process naturally leads to a surrender of the separate self, I found that there arose in my awareness on this occasion an extra gesture: a willful participation in that surrender by "offering" my awareness—my being, in fact—to all arising phenomena. That is, I was not only becoming still, or empty, in the field of arising experience. There was also an active intent to increase mindfulness with regard to all peripheral awareness. Or to *dedicate* the imaginary "center" of awareness to the wide totality of arising perceptions, as if to stretch the skin of self-consciousness into non-existence. Awareness itself was actively "upholding" the appearance, the diversity, and the particularness of all things, allowing consciousness to attentively affirm the virtue and integrity of each thing to be what it is, and to be fully recognized in the light of awareness. This in itself became a fusing of the field of oneness and the field of diversity, of the field of absolute awareness and the field of relative experience, and of the field of love and the field of emptiness. In sum, I see now as I write this, it was a gesture of love—the dedication of the "self" to "others."

Not meaning to overstate my capacity for such a practice, this was the nature of my meditation as the final bell rang and the retreat concluded on the morning of the tenth day. Master Sheng Yen stood before us and offered some concluding remarks, which I do not recall except for one word that stuck in my mind as he spoke. It was the word "relinquish." Then the bells and drums began for the concluding service, the chanting of various sutras, vows, prayers, and dedications.

As the chanting began, I experienced a strange sensation. It was the sensation that my body was made of sand, and that the wind was gently blowing all the sand away. This was shortly followed by the sensation of a ripple in the air, or a shimmer in the fabric of being. I recognized it as the sensation that a major revelation—an enlightenment experience—was about to occur. In the instantaneous space of thought, the following three thoughts arose. First, in the sudden excitement of that sensation, came the grasping thought, "Oh, I really want that!" This was followed by the word "relinquish" arising in my mind. And that was followed instantaneously by the sincere relinquishment of my grasping for experience or for any desire of accumulation to myself. Recognizing in that moment that the accumulation of self-enhancing experience, or the desire for it, was itself a dead end, I surrendered my grasping of experience to a humble confidence and faith in the nature of reality, independent of a personal reference. I trusted only in what reality intended, now or ever. It was the Buddhist equivalent of "Thy will be done." And simultaneous with that, the fabric tore, and the universe turned inside out.

Whereas a moment before there had been separate beings collectively engaged in chanting—the sound arising from within us—now there was only the ocean of Being itself, continually welling up as the world of appearance. The chant was arising from the heart of that ocean, not from, but through, separate beings who were only the froth on the waters. To perceive that anything originated or proceeded from separate beings was only an illusion of the mind. It was like believing that foam on the ocean was the source of the ocean's activity, rather than the most superficial expression of that activity.

The perspective of my awareness continued to widen and deepen from "foam" consciousness to ocean consciousness, as if awareness was being drawn "upstream" to the source of all consciousness and manifestation. Quickly my awareness was prior to the manifestation of all worlds, and was both *in the presence of* and *the same as* the original vast and loving impulse of creation and manifestation. And this awareness was arising not in another reality, but here, even as I continued chanting, gazing at times at the alive and awake eyes of the Buddha on the altar, which seemed to gaze back with that same ocean consciousness.

In a story that I wrote several months later, I tried to capture some of the experience in these words:

> *It was as if the bottom dropped out of the story of existence, and a great timeless ocean of reality washed ashore in its place. A golden sea of eternity forever chanting its own name. And out of this chanting arose all possibilities and all creation—the appearance of in and out, up and down, good and bad, and my own self . . . spinning my own stories, identifying with them, and shrinking to whatever-size character was required of me by the tale.*
>
> *But now, as I allowed myself to relinquish my hold on life, my attention was released back again to behold the marvelous source. And the source was in no way ever hidden, nor had I ever left it, but was always arising and ever present as what things are, simply shining out in every moment and every event without exclusion. In this openness I found myself embracing all of existence while seeing right through it like glass. The complete and simple reality of all things was by virtue of their very emptiness, their non-fixity as anything other than this same shining source, the whole and the each forever giving birth to each other. And I saw that from the very beginning of no-time there was only the one Giver and the one Receiver and the one Gift, and they were all the same one. One primal bodhisattva intimately serving the nothingness of his own creation. And I was that. We all are.*

Perhaps I should have been overwhelmed, but instead I was simply at home in creation for the first time, to the farthest reaches of the galaxies, and on either side of "life" and "death."

As I felt myself drawn into the dimension of the all-knowing, all-loving and creative source, it was now "personified" for me as a beautiful and androgynous "young man" of masculine and feminine natures. I knew that what I was looking at was the primordial Buddha, or primordial bodhisattva energy. This being was strangely familiar to me. I saw into his heart and soul, and into his motivating power. It was as if I were in "his" presence and totally aware of "him," while at the same time realizing that I *was* he.

THE INNOCENCE OF CREATION

Before I further recount the subjective details of my experience, and of the impressions that stayed with me, allow me to offer a bit of context. The archetypal qualities of Being remain philosophical abstractions unless embodied in our own experience. As these qualities are living qualities, they may also be embodied in a personification that helps transmit the nature of these qualities to our human psyche. These personifications arise not only as our ordinary or naive mental projections. They appear to arise as well in an *imaginal* (not imaginary) realm at the deepest level of spiritual experience, even to advanced practitioners of non-theistic paths. We see them in all the personifications of Mahayana and Vajrayana Buddhism—not just as symbols, but as supra-physical relationships, in which non-conceptual truths are conveyed to the psyche. Sometimes this can be quite playful. Why not? These are not literal or reified gods, nor are they popular mythology or superstition. They are real and living experiences of, and a living relationship to, the primordial realities of being, personified at the depths of our psyche.

In Vajrayana, the primordial reality is sometimes personified as the relationship of the primordial beings Samantabhadra and

Samantabhadri, the masculine/feminine marriage of primordial *awareness* and primordial *creative manifestation*—who are aspects of one being, one reality. And what Buddhism describes as the so-called *sambhogakaya* Buddhas, such as Vajrasattva or Vajradhara (often depicted as noble youths), are understood as emanations of the primordial awareness of Samantabhadra, able to transmit this awareness to human adepts. In sum, they embody the *threefold* reality of the divine play, or the three bodies (*kayas*) of the Buddha: the empty creative ground (*dharmakaya*), the luminous transmissive power (*sambhogakaya*), and the human embodiment (*nirmanakaya*). In Christianity, the luminous manifestations of the Christ, or of the Holy Mother, which may appear in mystical visions, have similar relational reality.

I assume this sort of very specific personification arose for me as a way of embodying to my awareness the essential and beloved qualities of the Creative Ground of Being. And as I want to be true to conveying my direct experience—or at least how it made me feel—in accurate detail, and not just abstractly, I will risk painting for you this picture of Creative Being with quirky and playful familiarity.

My impression of divine creative being, the very personification of Buddha-nature, was of One of a noble princely nature—like a young man so innocent, so good, that he is incapable of any gainful employment other than to create and redeem the universe out of his love. In the fable, he'd be the kid everyone shakes their heads at. His parents can't get him to learn a trade. He spends his time wandering off into the woods creating universes of love. But all of the qualities of the Creative Ground were manifest in this youth.

I saw that his goodness, his love, and his creative power are *synonymous*. His love *must* create, and his love *must* love. It is the very nature of his love to manifest as *that which is to be loved;* so that it *can* be loved, and so that it may unfold as his love to the final consummation of that love. Only in this does that love find full expression. It is the complete actuality of *One Reality* manifesting as the play of relationship, which is the expression of love.

I wish I could convey the oceanic, or orchestral, majesty of the overall experience. On the other hand, I also need to somehow convey the humble familiarity of my sensing of this divine reality. So imagine the nicest guy you might have known in high school—if you were lucky. Maybe he wore a varsity sweater. But he was no common jock. (And this is where the maternal, or feminine, prevails.) He was affable, intelligent, kind, generous, mature, compassionate, and a friend to all. So innocent that he couldn't help but create worlds out of his love, just so he could love them—even as he walked down the school corridors! It was his nature and passion. It was as if God—or this celestial Buddha—was already my (and everyone's) best friend and benefactor before the creation itself. But I also knew myself to *be* him—and an extension of his own creative awareness, power, and love manifesting into the created world.

I should clarify here that, for all this elaborated detail of imagery and personification, this was not a visual experience of being in a strange realm with another being. It was a shift within consciousness itself, a progressive subjective knowing. It was the explicitness of that knowing that suggested or simultaneously translated into the mind as the detailed characterization portrayed above.

Witnessing the love, the impulse to create, and the act of creation as one event, I felt myself as identical to, and none other than, a ray of that love; an expression of the Source participating in creation as a full commitment to, and involvement in, that which was being created. And hence I, as He, also entered into the realm (and role) of the created. I watched myself as a "ray of this light" entering into the earth creation, embodying the full spectrum of vibration of his being, and being entirely an expression of his compassionate love and awareness, his eyes and his hands on the earth—not as a separate being, but purely as an expression of his committed love.

I saw how the full spectrum of love and awareness could get entangled in these lower vibrating feedback loops of dualistic awareness that characterized the creation, and become captivated and distracted there for eons. I saw my capacity for ignorance. I saw that it would be difficult not to identify with the relative contexts of experience, and lose my originating awareness. And yet that distorted awareness *was the very same awareness,* and the very same being, as that of the Source—or the "father," as Jesus frames it—purely expressing as "me."

I saw how my consciousness always had the capacity, and the option, of remembering, of awakening; of making "the full father shift," as I began playfully calling it in the years to come, enjoying its alliteration. That was my name for the ability to instantaneously shift perspective, to relax the dualistic consciousness and its compounded reactivities, and to allow the stream of original, or source, consciousness to subsume it. To recognize in the moment that I was empty *of* a separate self; and empty *to* that river of loving consciousness. That "I and the Father are One."

IGNORANCE, EVOLUTION, AND AGENCY

I seemed to witness, from the perspective of the Creator's heart, the dynamic by which the created is identical to the creator, yet manifesting *relatively* as a separate creation (otherwise it would be no creation at all). It totally participates in the nature of God, yet it is God in the aspect of a self-project that God can support and love—even root for, you might say. It is not a cruel, or even neutral, manipulation from the outside. It is a natural and inevitable expression of the involvement, or involution, of Creative Goodness.

But here is the play in the delicate realm of paradox: the *creation* is the expression of all of God's consciousness and all of God's creative power, and yet the *created* is subject to the distraction of its own relative form. *God's consciousness,* inherent in the created—now playfully modified through the structures of duality—perceives, at the level of human consciousness, a sense of its own separation. And God's creative power, still inherent in that relative consciousness, enables it to respond by creating its own mental worlds, or stories—especially the story of its own separated selfhood or ego—*as a solution to the separation.*

This creates a virtual split in consciousness from the recognition that we, the divine reality, exist not only within, but as, the field of reciprocity with all things; that our own nature *is* the dynamic reciprocity of love. Apart from that reciprocity, there is no "self." *As* that reciprocity, we are the self of inexhaustible non-exclusiveness. This is the Buddhist meaning of *emptiness,* or of *interbeing,* as Thich Nhat Hanh refers to it. To presume to nurture a self-interest independent of that reciprocity is the ultimate dead end that our human species may be facing on this planet. That recognition and understanding is most keenly preserved in the wisdom of our indigenous peoples, and it is calling to us today.

Freud pointed out that the ego arises in tandem with the inability of the infant consciousness to accept the loss of the mother—that nourishing field of eros and oneness. We could as well say that our consciousness suffers the loss of experiencing our intrinsic Divine Wholeness. In the trauma of that loss, the essential dimension of *reciprocity,* the truth of *interbeing,* is replaced by the project of becoming "complete in ourselves"—that is, complete within our own self image. Paradoxically, the ego is our first stumbling solution to the desire to recreate wholeness. But as an ultimately false solution—an early and necessary experiment, we might say—it only reinforces separation.

As humans, we are indeed created in the image of consciousness, love, and creative choice. But working within a relative field of perception, we tend to make different, and relatively deluded, creative choices—choices that perpetuate our perception of separation rather than helping to clarify our true nature. Yet we are capable of greater insight.

From within the relative realm of time and space and historical perception, it is possible to study scientifically the evolving complexity of living forms, the evolution of human consciousness, the trials and errors of that consciousness, and our ultimate capacity to choose a path of conscious awakening as pointed to by the wisdom traditions. This is all part of our story. But beneath that story is the inherently compassionate and awakened Heart/Mind of Being ever unfolding and supporting us. Our evolution in awareness is facilitated or retarded by how we learn to recognize and respond to life's lessons. That is, our development depends upon whether we learn to use life's routine undermining of the ego's pretensions as an opportunity to *reinforce* past conditioning or as an opportunity to *relinquish* past conditioning; as an opportunity for embellishing our story or as an opportunity for paying attention.

The underlying truth has never been separate from us. We are the immediacy and fullness of God's creative consciousness and love here and now, either awakened to Itself or not; either Self-realized or not; making choices that express our awakening or not. Deluded or not, we are intrinsically empowered to awaken as co-creators of the fullness of this reality of *loving fully and of being loved.* All of which we ourselves Are.

Does this conjure the image of the avatar? The term is usually used to refer to the conscious incarnation of a deity. But we are all sleeping avatars with the potential to awaken. It is not the ego that is the avatar. The ego is the sleep. Nor is it the ego that awakens. God awakens. Primordial wisdom rediscovers itself. We are each embodiments of the several-fold nature of Being, or God. The nature of God, the nature of Creation, and the nature of God present in creation is one reality—and that is love. And that is what each of us is.

We need not say "God." The word is not meant to reify a deity or a self. But I am comfortable with that word as warmly referring to the holistic and holographic nature of reality, which is inherently alive, conscious, creative, and relational. And which does not thereby inadvertently suggest anything purely technical, or less than the personhood and ultimate fullness of our own humanity. We could equally quote Buddhist terminology to point to the *self-arising pristine awareness* and *universal creativity* inherent to *pure and total presence.* And to explain that all arising appearance—all creation—is one with, not other than, the *integrative structure of pure and total presence;* the *fundamental space of being;* the *awake and empty potential that is all-responsive;* the *ceaseless compassion in which being-for-others is always available.* In either case, our egoic dream is merely a distortion—our misperception—of that conscious loving presence that is our essential nature.

Through the contractive and separative lens of the ego, our essential Presence is identified and championed as our separate self-identity and egoic survival. Our essential Awareness is identified with the world built up of our thoughts and projections. And, in keeping with this screen of separate identity and reactive thinking, our essential capacity as love is expressed as the full scale of our reactive emotions. We are fully incarnated as the sleep of consciousness.

Yet when that illusory distortion of separation and contraction relaxes, we find ourselves expressing not as a *functional contraction,* but as the *essential radiance* of creation, that same avataric energy that has never separated from its original nature as love. Our full feeling, energy, and awareness again flows out to the world.

From a Western nineteenth-century dualistic standpoint, Freud believed our instinctual life energy—seeing its expression only in self-possessed sexual or destructive urges—would create chaos unless restricted by the ego, and sublimated to cultural ends. In this view, all we can hope for, at best, is a rational compromise between pleasure and reality. He had no context for recognizing that the awakening and mature integration of our true nature, beyond the self-possession of the ego, releases the radiant nature of our life energy from egoic contraction, allowing it to flow back into the world as the pleasure and joy of being, as the fullness of responsive caring, as unobstructed seeing, and as the power of love.

What we experience as our suffering or as our happiness is already the complete expressiveness of God's Being beyond and within time. We are never other than that Wholeness which manifests and loves right through the creation, through all the distortions of finite experience to full self-realization as love again. And *our* subjective journey— our individual awakening as love in dedication to the creation—is *that* subjective journey. It is the awakening of our avataric nature. Then we do not see ourselves as victims of anything; nor are we hoping for salvation. Rather, we *are* the salvation awakening to its capacity to love, and learning to take responsibility for loving.

LOVE AND AWAKENING

As I leave as a ray of the supreme love and enter into the Earth, I feel the powerful possibilities and likelihood of falling asleep in the created realm, even as I know the absolute truth of my God function and the task of its constant reawakening. Even as God makes this constant "sacrifice," I make that sacrifice. I am the Source. I am the Process of love's dedication. I am the Awakening.

Though all of this is true in an eternal moment—this union of lover and beloved—we experience this process projected as time, and as drama. In that drama, love flows ever downward, like water flowing into the tiniest places. In the Christian language, the holy spirit is the aspect of God's love moving into the heart of creation, flowing like water to bring the mercy of love and awakening. In Buddhist language, it is bodhicitta, the awakened heart nature of the universe entering into the heart of all our activity in dedication to our awakening. In dedication to others.

As bodhicitta/holy spirit awakens in us—as our own nature awakens in us—we find ourselves to *be* the very water of love seeping into all those tight spaces where only water can seep: the tight spaces of grief, fear, pain, hatred, and persecution; and of the suffering generated by our ignorant responses in the most mundane circumstances of our lives and our relationships. We are committed to being awake and available. That is what it is to be fully embodied in this life. To recognize who it is that is embodied. To understand the nature of this embodiment. To be the body of existence beneath the story of existence.

It does not guarantee an easy path. It does not make anyone special. It does not promise to bypass a broken heart. It does not offer facile salvific predictions about human politics or history. It does not guarantee the return of our species to harmony with the living organism of Earth, which is itself the full embodiment of God's beauty and intelligence. It does not assure that the determined roadster of our love will make it across the track just ahead of the barreling freight train of our ignorance.

But it offers us the true fruit of each moment. It offers the salvation of our moment-to-moment commitment and awakening; to the conscious reciprocity that allows for genuine acknowledgement of each other; to the emptiness, or humility, that allows for the renewal of human possibility; to our persistence as love despite all evidence to the contrary. This is the moment-to-moment salvation that we beautiful human beings have proved capable of now and throughout our history. It is ahistorical. It is the expression of what we are.

And still the water seeps, and love loves. And we make the choices that allow us to stand clear in our self nature, and to uphold others in their self nature; continuing like water through all states and stages, until it has sought through to its lowest level, its common denominator. And that common denominator is love.

Drink and You Will See

Like you, I once thought
I was a tiny creature in this vast
creation. Now, I'd like to
offer you this magnificent display,
the moon and the stars, served
in this ancient clay teapot and steeped
for just the right amount of
time. Drinking it,
you will see that you are also
the host or hostess of all the created
worlds; the gracious server
of all tea; the mother of the universe
laughing in your womb; the
best of friends.

PART TWO

When Our Life Becomes the Path

The awakening above is produced only in response to the awakening below, for the awakening above depends upon the longing/desire of that below.

THE ZOHAR (VOL. 1, 86B)

Recently, one friend asked, "How can I force myself to smile when I am filled with sorrow? It isn't natural." I told her we must be able to smile to our sorrow because we are more than sorrow. . . . Smiling means that we are ourselves, that we have sovereignty over ourselves, that we are not drowned in forgetfulness. . . . When we say, "I take refuge in the Buddha," we should also understand that "The Buddha takes refuge in me," because without the second part the first part is not complete. The Buddha needs us for awakening, understanding, and love to be real things, and not just concepts.

THICH NHAT HANH

Fairy Tale

"And it came to pass," said the dwarf,
"that the characters in the tale,
grown dubious of its origins, and doubtful
of the author's intentions—and even
of his lonely capacity to realize them;
and having grasped at last that
the tale was about nothing but their own
being—awoke and bore witness to themselves,
and told a tale that bespoke their
truest nature; and with great
tenderness brought to pass a wonderful
work, the likes of which had never
been seen between the pages of a book."

"My Good Dwarf," said the princess,
"is it not enough that you have helped me
out of the well that you must now
tempt me out of the tale as well? And
would it not be the last act of hubris—
and a desperate separation—that we
declare ourselves independent of that
great intelligence that authored us,
and apart from which we are meaning-
less fragments?"

"Just so, My Princess. And just so
does that true power enter into the very
tale, governing no longer by the illusion
of overweening design, but empowering
its players directly, by that same

intelligence, to step out of chapter
and verse into that boundless clear air
in which the choice to love knows nothing
of scripture nor of law, nor of the logic
of the tale; and in which every act,
naked at last under starlight, is
homage to that great being of love
whom they themselves are, and only in
whom is the tale resolved."

And the princess grew faint at first,
but consented to be helped
from the well, and traveled with the
dwarf down the road to the castle;
all the while pulling at the straps of her
gown, which, it seemed to her now,
was a few sizes too small.

Memos to Myself

❀

We have agreed to pause here together in the gentle air of the late afternoon sun. We have agreed to share this moment of mutual seeing without the need to project or to hide. Our deepening silence together brings deepening recognition. We begin to apprehend in each other, and between us, something greater and more all-inclusive than our apparent selves. We are held in the lap of a greater coherence, felt inwardly and between us as a conscious loving presence. It is our participation in the divine mystery of beholder and beheld, the dance within God's own being, the communion of basic space and awareness—Samantabhadri and Samantabhadra—that is the body of reality. And it is also the clarification of our humanity and of our human relations.

The essentials of our awakening spiritual maturity are congruent with the essentials of our awakening psychological and emotional human maturity. What enables us to be awake and coherent in the community of the spirit is what allows us to be awake and functional within and as the human community. What enables me to enter into a humble, vulnerable, reciprocal, maturing, and awakened intimacy with God also enables me to be in humble, vulnerable, reciprocal, maturing, and awakened intimacy with you and my fellow humans—or, at least, in truly functional relationship.

We live what we experience as "a human existence on Earth." It is rewarding and challenging enough. But what is it? And what are we? How do we allow our own human existence to awaken to the full experience of what we are? And how do we enable our tormented human species to better avail itself of the empathy and love that is already wired into us as our organic potential?

When these questions become our path, then our path becomes our life. The familiar needn't become unfamiliar; in fact, it might become truly familiar for the first time. My own experience allowed me to see through conventional dualistic reality to a non-dual interpenetrating and embracing totality that is empty, unified, conscious, spontaneous, and relational. At the same time, I was shown that our conventional reality *is* that absolute reality experienced in relative terms. Our consciousness is a fractal, we might say, of God-consciousness. This very next moment is a fractal of eternity. And our whole earthly drama is a fractal of the paradox of "the absolute which expresses as the relative"— that is, the One which expresses as all of us, down to our last delusion— by its very nature.

In our relative ignorance, we not only experience this reality in accordance with our dualistic conditioning; we also learn to act in ways that perpetuate our dualistic experience and subsequent conditioning. Hence this realization calls on us to become both wise in our openness and our perception, and skillful in our actions; for only with both together do we generate a life that is coherent with the truth.

Delusion and suffering are not an accident or part of a poorly designed plan, nor the product of a separate "evil." They are intrinsic to the paradox of reality, but we must become wise to them. Julian of Norwich has Jesus saying essentially this in *Revelations of Divine Love.* Having experienced that sin is "empty," she asks Jesus why there had to be sin in the first place. And very tenderly, not going into a technical explanation, but as if explaining to a child, he says, "Just trust that it had to be this way. But you will see that all shall be well; that every conceivable thing shall be well." As if to say that "error" is an inevitable *artifact* of evolution, but not its *actual* nature. Which is what the Buddha's enlightenment experienced in the present tense—that the truth of all delusive manifestation *is* original goodness.

Thus, my own early vision revealed "every manner of thing" to be love only. It was Being apprehended in its "resurrected" aspect. God's nature is all-inclusive *by the very nature of love;* just as all the categories of dualism and suffering existence are recognized in Buddhism as *not other* than the underlying and loving spaciousness of being—which is capable of seeing itself in its fullness through our eyes.

Beyond the dualistic categories of pleasure and pain, good and evil, it is Love itself that is the unifying truth. Love is our business here. Not love that is merely sentimental; or an expression of our attachment. Love that is the simple and fierce affirmation of the life and integrity of others, and of all things. Love that incinerates the self-defeating tendency toward negativity, in all the pervasive ways that negativity arises within us. We might say that to persist as love despite all evidence to the contrary can only be the result of the awakening of wisdom. But such love also awakens wisdom. They are existentially one.

Is the ultimate goal then to awaken from this deluded world into a realm of ultimate enlightenment? The teachings of the fourteenth-century Tibetan sage, Tsongkhapa, among others, suggest that a realm of absolute realization, enlightenment, nirvana, or Buddhahood is not the true point. The idea of purifying all of the "goodness" from all of the "badness," or all of the enlightenment from all of the delusion, is just another dualistic delusion (and one perversely responsible for much of the suffering on this planet). Whereas "the mind of kindness," Tsongkhapa writes (in Lex Hixon's translation), "supremely skillful in loving care, unveils the infinite value of every single life, demonstrating *compassion* as *the meaning of existence*" (italics mine).*
The function of the Buddhas and the bodhisattvas is the activation of *compassion*. And it is suffering that activates compassion. Hence it is our familiar realm, the realm of suffering, that is the potent spiritual realm; and suffering beings are the mothers of the Buddhas. To persist as love despite all evidence to the contrary is, we may say, the mother of the "resurrection."

But since this paradox, and its resolution, exists in and *as* us, it is only our own path of walking that can distill and manifest this realization and this love. All our trials and our learning, all our devo-

---

*See Lex Hixon, *Mother of the Buddhas* (Wheaton, Il.: Quest Books, 1993), 239.

tion and our sacrifice, all our study and our practice, all our ordinariness and our uniqueness, all our silence and our surrender, all our joy and our laughter, are the experiencing and the awakening of the true nature of being.

Thus, our way is to walk that walk. And to avail ourselves of all the grace of the teaching that is built into and taught by the world around us (our daily bread), including the "wisdom teachings" and the practices as they come to us. But these teachings and practices will be most serviceable if we perceive them not only as *paths* to love, but also as *invitations* to love, moment to moment. Then we may learn, as Tsongkhapa expresses it, "to discriminate sensitively and unerringly between actions which negate the preciousness of others and actions which affirm and judiciously care for others."

My intention in these writings was to reaffirm the gracious reality and availability of direct experience as a source of spiritual understanding; to place my own experience in a wider context; and to reflect on the meanings such experiences have for our daily lives and how we may live our lives in availability to direct experience. My own experiences, and the fact that they were inclusive of so many different perspectives—personal and impersonal, theistic and non-theistic, all opening windows on the same greater reality—incline me to view all religious traditions—not the cultural dimension, but the wisdom dimension—as manifesting downstream from one greater truth that is their source. Each has a unique understanding and a unique poetry to offer us.

Looking back over this account, I could see how the intimations of my early years were fleshed out over a lifetime. And how the later occasions of direct witness underpin my life—even in its abject moments. I'd hate to be pinned to a reductive characterization of any of these foregoing experiences, which exist in their own light beyond words, and which each include or imply all the others. But if it were useful to touch lightly on the essential message of each experience—my sworn testimony—this is what I might say of each of the nine experiences cited earlier:

1. Fundamental reality is capable of knowing itself through us as a creative, intrapenetrating, and paradoxically inclusive totality of being, of which love is its very self-substance. That reality manifests my life, and is potentially knowable to me as my own unfolding surrender to the experiences of consciousness and love.

2. The totality—or simple truth—of that is in no way distinct from the moment-to-moment experience of my life and of myself. Although not usually perceived in that way by the relative structures of my mind, I wholly and fully participate in and as that Reality every moment.

3. That creative play of reality includes my capacity to choose to experience myself as less than what I am.

4. The shadows and projections of the resultant story are an illusory film continually shown through and obviated by the actual love-light of consciousness.

5. All created form exists in and as the absolute truth of the openness of that self-existent light—never fallen, never saved—the recognition of which inspires only our compassion, our generosity, our morality, our patience, our dedication, and our completeness.

6. Life is the intimacy of that with itself.

7. Our images and representations of life and death, so seemingly compelling, are all part of the shadow play of projection—whereas the love that awakens in us is already the complete reality, subject to neither life nor death.

8. We are capable of the ultimate karma yoga, which is living and acting the expression of this truth in our lives; gyani yoga, which is perceiving our identity with the non-dual reality; and bhakti yoga, which is enjoying, surrendering, and absorbing into the love relationship with our own Source as the Beloved.

9. I am the very manifestation and Self of the Source, and its love play of creation, which engenders my own ignorance, separation,

and projections; but which empowers my reawakening to the full dimension of my true being, which is the selfless and creative edge of love-dedication to all being.

These were certainly extraordinary moments. But extraordinary experiences are not in themselves the point. They are only serviceable if they call our attention to the extraordinariness of this moment. The moment calls on all our God capacity to be awake, and to care for others and every aspect of creation around us. This is our field of conscious loving presence. That may sound like some distinct spiritual realm. But it is the very field of our vulnerability and of our tenderness. Of our reciprocity. And it plays itself out even in our mammalian embodiment, and in the dynamics of our emotional life. I may have a deep insight, or even profoundly direct experience, of a transcendent reality. But if that is not to be a dead piece of baggage, I must allow it to bring me back to the lip of unknowing, to an availability, and to an offering of myself, over and over again.

The question before us then is: How do we actually maintain an open field of trust, tenderness, vulnerability, and reciprocity ("become like little children")—a field in which we can truly grow and mature—amidst the dynamics of an emotional and instinctual life that would often have us shutting down, dismissing, protecting, judging, fixating, and attacking? This question, and this dynamic, applies equally to our relationship to ourselves, to others, and to our greater life, or to God. If we are, as it is sometimes said, "spiritual beings having a human experience," then we must honor the vulnerable dynamics of our emotional and spiritual growth at the human level, and the exploratory tenderness of our human experience.

Of course, centuries of literature have been directed to this question, and I won't attempt to reproduce it. I would just like to offer a memorandum of some things that I have studied and found useful over a lifetime, and on a day-to-day basis, that are most relevant to us today, taking note of themes highlighted by my own recorded experiences in part one of this book, and others that have arisen for me as useful companions and perspectives. And when I also address the Buddhist and Christian "dharmas" below, I am not presuming to speak with an orthodox voice, but rather I am embracing these teachings in my own experience, and affirming in a universal and poetic way the wonderful companionship and support of all spiritual traditions.

In Me the Universe

In me the universe
presumes to be lover and friend.
In me the universe hovers
at the choice point between love and fear,
to bless or to withdraw. I am the one
who hovers here. I am the one who speaks
from the heart of what we are.
Shall we agree not to disown our selves
and the voice that speaks us? Here,
where the stars are just emerging in our dusk
and playful darkness settles like a cat
on the rooftops; where the river lights
are gleaming, and rose and jasmine
perfume the courtyard: shall we not convene
our ancient mariachi band, when
there are so many eager and waiting
to dance into the night? Oh friend,
pick up your divine instrument.
I am the one who calls to you
from what you are.

Vulnerability

One can take a "samurai" attitude to enlightenment—and there is everything to be said for arousing clear focus, fierce energy, and determination. But these must be imbued with a gentle humility and tenderness that can work its way down through the cracks in our armor and our pain, rather than inadvertently stiffening them. We must embrace our vulnerability if we are to have enlightenment embrace us. To embrace, but not to wallow, is its own kind of fierceness.

There is a wonderful Zen story about a samurai who comes to a Zen master and says, "Please explain to me the nature of heaven and hell." The master replies, "Why should I waste my time trying to explain such subtle truths to a crude and ignorant person like you?" The samurai rises up in fury, draws his sword, and says, "How dare you speak to me like that! I could as easily cut your head off right now!" "*That,*" says the master, looking up, "is hell." The samurai realizes what the master is teaching him, and bows his head, kneeling before the master in apology. "And that," says the master, "is heaven."

Whatever the spiritual abstractions or the metaphysics that arise for us, they are played out simply in the tenderness of our human lives. We can speak in purely traditional spiritual terms; but if we are to start at our human center, and not bypass the heart of our vulnerability, then we must honor the child in us. It is in our infancy and childhood that the neural pathways that embody our capacity for attunement, empathy, and compassion are laid down. They are nurtured in the raw moments of communion and reciprocity between child and mother. And as long as that capacity for reciprocity is sustained, we are at rest in our empathetic relation to life.

Our empathy circuits are whole-body circuits that help us to attune both to the reality of self and to the reality of the other. But the developmental circumstances of our lives will inevitably trigger us, even traumatize us, out of that innocent communion into the mental circuitry and structures of separation, projection, identification, strategy, and survival. (I define "trauma" here, in the broadest sense, as any experience that overwhelms our empathy circuits such that we must disconnect from those circuits and from our own felt wholeness of being.) Depending on traumatic or nurturing influences, these reactive structures will be ever more defended as our adult structures; or they will mature into adult capacities for empathy, wholeness, intimacy, and integration.

As long as we identify with a virtual image of a separate self, we naturally circle the wagons around that vulnerable construction, while both defending and denying its vulnerability. But as we learn to bring a tender sense of presence to perceiving and acknowledging that vulnerability, we also begin to open the door to the inherent reciprocity and intimacy of our experience, and to the spontaneity of our participation in the flow of life. And our attention is turned not to the imaginary film—the stories that create, explain, or justify how we feel or how we act—but to the healing intimacy of aware presence, and empathy with the feelings themselves. In this way our mental/emotional states are not triggered and played out in the endless movie of separate selfhood, but rather are subsumed in the liberating reality of awareness and presence that is our own essential wholeness of being prior to the perception and defense of a vulnerable separation.

This is the marriage of our child capacity for innocence and openness with our adult capacity for a mature and integrating healing presence, which together optimize the creative journey to our mature possibility. The alternative is to rely on our neurotic adaptations, which become the specialized forms of our cognitive and emotional limitations.

Such "specializations" inhibit any further evolutionary development in an individual; whereas the open and non-fixated range of our childhood holds the key not only to the evolution of our own maturity, but to the evolution of the species as well.

I'd like to dwell on this last point for a moment, for it is easy to pass by. This model of childhood holding the key to our evolution is a truth that reveals itself to us on many levels. It is a principle, if I may be briefly technical, recognized even in the field of physical anthropology, where it is termed *neoteny,* or *paedomorphosis.* It correlates the evolutionary development of primates with the length of time the infant or child qualities and features persist into adult development. This is even observed physically and skeletally. If you look at images of the fetuses of all primate species, you will see they closely resemble the human fetus. At birth, the skull and physical proportions look the closest to human children; yet each goes through a skeletal morphosis according to its genetically adapted needs. The shape of the skull, and the body ratios, go from looking like a baby human to looking like an adult gorilla, for example. This subsequent *specialization* of the childhood form gives it certain advantages within its niche; yet it is less universal overall in its adaptive capacities. The human form, on the other hand, barely changes from its fetal equivalent as a baby ape. In not specializing, it carries the widest adaptive potential for its evolutionary line.

Similarly with cognitive and behavioral development, those species that have the longest childhood and childhood dependency have the richest sustained opportunity for reciprocity and for cultural learning, and hence the widest adaptive potential. The same is true for our emotional and spiritual development. The more we are able to preserve and carry the natural qualities of healthy childhood—such as innocence, openness, reciprocity, playfulness, curiosity, creativity, spontaneity—into our maturity, the more we are able to fulfill the creative possibilities of that maturity, including the spiritual possibilities. And, says the noted anthropologist Ashley Montagu most enticingly, "It may also stimulate the beginning of new cascades of macroevolutionary transformations."*

So to relax our inner adult posturing and simply stay attuned to the child within us begins to hold open a wonderful space for our understanding and our evolution. There is a wonderful story about Mr. (Fred) Rogers recounted by reporter Tom Junod in his December 2019 article in *The Atlantic,* "My Friend Mr. Rogers": "When I first visited the Neighborhood 21 years ago, one of his in-house writers, Hedda Sharapan, told me what had happened when he'd enlisted her to write a manual intended to teach doctors how to talk to children. She worked hard on it, using all her education and experience in the field of child development, but when she handed him her opening, he crossed out what she'd written and replaced it with six words: 'You were a child once too.'"

---

*See Ashley Montagu, *Growing Young* (New York, Ny.: McGraw-Hill, 1983).

Nurture and Nature

*I*t is true, in an important sense, that we must become like little children, and childlike in our contemplation, if we are to "enter the kingdom of heaven"—if we are to rediscover the field of our original being, of our conscious loving presence—which is the beginning, as well as the mature end, of our human possibility. A fully mature adult embodies the tenderness, simplicity, and openness of a child. In contrast, our so-called adulthood is characterized by defensive patterns that prevent our childhood structures from ever reaching wholeness or maturity.

I may at times find myself asking a client, "If you gave yourself permission to feel and speak as a child right now, how would you express your needs?" I ask this not to reinforce a childhood need structure, but rather because most of our so-called adult needs are, in fact, imbued with continuations and projections of unfulfilled child needs. Our unconscious defenses, and our denial of this fact, are responsible for most of our dysfunctional and self-destructive adaptations to life on this planet: our hungers and our resentments, our disregard and our violence to ourselves and others, our everyday pain and lack of fulfillment.

How then might a child, with adult language, respond to this question of needs and wants? I want love. I want to be fed or nourished. I want to be seen and known. I want to feel connected. I want to feel safe. I want to be free to express myself and my love. I want to be heard. I want to feel full and substantial. I want relief. I want to feel at One. As mammals, we are all keyed to the experience of being bonded with, and nurtured by, the mother. Our bodies know what to expect. And they know when that expectation has not been realized or has been lost. Even at best, such direct bonding is a provisional arrangement that must transition into new forms of maturity. But from womb to breast to responsive mothering, such bonding is our first and primordial experience of the field of conscious loving presence while in our embodied life.

The early loss of awareness of our essential self, and identification with the body and with separation, is an inevitable dynamic. Hence it is not my intention here to argue for a utopian vision of a culture of perfect parenting or of "perfect childhood." That in itself will not solve the human dilemma of separation and survival in an embodied existence in a seemingly threatening and material world—although it would give us the optimal foundation nature intended and allows. My intention here is simply to point to a key structure of human experience. It is founded on loss and our response to loss. And we need to embrace this consciously and lovingly as we unfold the full creative play of our human faculties.

For our mammalian embodiment, the deep bond of emotional and physical nurturance by the nursing mother is a naturally privileged and temporary extension of our pre-birth unity and fulfillment—the comprehensive connectedness and nurturance of the womb. And it is an extension we are not all granted. The experience of being bathed in the mother's attention, and in her heart-field, while ingesting the pure total nourishment of her warm milk, is nothing less than divine ecstasy—a sense of warmth, nourishment, and complete sufficiency that pervades everywhere in the body and in the consciousness. Every system in the body is opening to its own divine dance of growth, integration, unfoldment, and reciprocity. In response to sustained eye-contact, the attunement pathways of the brain and nervous system are growing new fibers and unfolding with the capacity for self-attunement and attunement with others. We are buoyed for our journey into the sea of experience, and for our inevitable reactive and contractive adaptations to the stress of life. This is our divine incarnated moment that some of us never experience, and all of us lose all too soon. It is also an occasion that may be admixed with inconsistency and varied emotional messages, as our caretakers do not perfectly embody that divine presence, but rather express their own adaptive conditioning to the stress of life.

It could be said that all of our addictive inclinations—inclinations that to one extent or another define much of our adult human functioning—are the organism's attempt to restore a sense of aliveness, connectedness, sufficiency, or peace that our adaptations to life have not otherwise been able to retain. This includes not only our addiction to grossly self-destructive external substances, used in an effort to restore that divine milieu. It includes not only our addiction to hormone-stimulating behaviors—relational, sexual, thrill-seeking, power, and others. It includes not only our addiction to everyday arousers, soothers, or numbers. Ironically, it especially includes our addiction to our neurotic defensive systems, to the denial of real feelings and needs, to compulsive thinking and reactive emotion, to a fixated sense of self or ego, to the need to be right, and to all of our projective systems that actually reinforce and maintain the experience of separation. In sum, they are the activities of traumatized children not knowing how to own or to integrate our actual experience.

Hence, the order of the world, as we know it, is an elaborate and complex acting-out of the trauma of our separation from the empathic field of conscious loving presence. And until we are able to surrender our defensive posturing and return to the scene of the loss—our childlike innocence and vulnerability—we will be hard put to find the doorway back into the "kingdom," or the openness required to walk through it.

Because much of our worldly conditioning is designed to adapt, compensate, substitute for, or deny our actual condition—our perceived loss and our reinforcement of that loss—we are always "missing the mark." This is the Greek term translated as "sin" in the English-language bible. Our "sin" is thus our patterns of thinking and behavior that inadvertently reinforce and entrench our sense of separation from the Field. In contrast, to fundamentally shift our psychological point of view—translated in the English bible as "repentance"—re-allows that childlike innocence that is open to new possibility, to the possibility of recognizing and re-embracing as present something we believed was lost: *love here and now*. And what we seem to have lost is not just some provisional experience in our childhood history. That is but a reflection within a larger dynamic. What we have lost is the very ground experience of our being, our Buddha-nature, the reality of conscious loving presence that embraces and transcends the circumstances of embodied life.

For the "good news" is that the lost kingdom, the field of conscious loving presence, is not the province of a distant or separate God, or of a church or temple hierarchy. Nor is it the exclusive property of our mothers to offer or withhold. Nor is it an idealization or a fantasy. Nor is it a distant accomplishment, or a reward for good behavior. It is the inherent field of our own being. It is "what we are made of." Conscious loving presence, intimate wholeness of being, even amidst the "fang and claw" of phenomena, is simply what the universe looks like from the inside. And we are spiritually disposed, as well as structurally enabled, to experience it.

It is the nature of embodiment itself—to be born as an individual body in an apparently dualistic and material world of finite dimensions—that is the fundamental existential or spiritual challenge. There is an inevitable journey of separation and rediscovered union that we are *structurally designed to be capable of making*. Our evolved brain/body organisms are structurally disposed to be able to experience and respond—instinctually and with growing wisdom—to the challenges of separation and to the challenges of survival. We are equipped to analyze, associate, project, make sense of, reason, and otherwise intuit or gain insight into our life situation. And, ultimately, spiritually as well as psychologically, we have the capacity to directly access and apprehend increasingly integrated patterns, and widening fields of information, that embrace and transcend our provisional separative perceptions, so that we may relocate ourselves within the non-material and unitive context of conscious loving presence. This is our mature spiritual potential.

We are not born as the mature accomplishment of our developmental potential. We are born as vulnerable and dependent beings into a relational field requiring nurturance and reciprocity. The development of our human faculties must begin in a dependent condition, and the quality of our early bonding, nurturance, support, and healthy attachment will have everything to do with the success of our integrated development as we move through the natural stages of maturation, from nurtured to nurturer.

The separation from the originally dependent experience of conscious loving presence in childhood is inevitable. And human beings have certainly demonstrated their capacity to overcome early deficits in order to make healing choices toward consciousness, love, and presence. Our childhoods are part of a larger pattern of our own conscious development, not deterministic in an absolute sense. However, the optimal use of our faculties in evolving a life in which consciousness, love, and presence are still paramount will be encouraged by optimal support and reciprocity during the stages of our organic dependency.

When these organic developmental needs have been suitably met, we will most naturally evolve that healthy independence that allows us to assume responsibility for our lives, including primary responsibility for our own feeling states. This means, above all, *assuming responsibility* for our felt states of separation and for the way we act out and maintain states of separation, rather than projecting blame onto the past or onto situations in the present. This is a profound and uncommon stage of psychological maturity that could also be deemed spiritual. For although in our dependent and immature stage we cannot be responsible for maintaining the integrity and reciprocity of the field of conscious loving presence, as mature adults we are entirely responsible. The pain, loss, fear, or overwhelm we experienced when our adult caretakers or culture were incapable of maintaining the reciprocal field led us to deny or withdraw from our own field of being, to further reify a separate self, or to *solidify* our natural tendency to withdraw—and to adopt compensatory and protective behaviors that inadvertently reinforce and maintain our sense of separation from the all-embracing field that includes ourselves and others.

This then is the pain we suffer, not through the loss of the field, but through the loss of our ability to experience the field. We could define all mature growth work, and all true spiritual discipline, as the steps we take to recognize and release our own mechanisms of separation, and to re-allow and reestablish our relationship to, even our identity with, the field of Conscious Loving Presence. This is not philosophy. This is who we are.

Reciprocity

Our vulnerability reminds us that we are never truly independent, but always exist in a field of reciprocity. Thus reciprocity is a deep spiritual principle. And its understanding also arises in the context of any mature and intact culture that has preserved wise counsel as to how we should function in human community. (Unfortunately, to find examples of purely reciprocal social models, we must look to some of the indigenous cultures that are vanishing in the wake of our hyper-individualism.) Hence the Nguni Bantu philosophy of *ubuntu,* and its teaching of *umuntu ngumuntu ngabantu,* which translates as "a person is a person through other persons," or "because we are, I am." Or the Tzutzujil Maya term, *kas-limaal,* which refers to the mutuality by which we enliven, or light the spark, in each other—and which also translates as a profound mutual indebtedness.

This is not only enlightened social philosophy. It is true right down to the level of our neurobiology. As we have said, the neural network that allows us to directly experience our own felt sense of self is activated by our first experience of eye contact and attunement to others. Stated again, this inner "social" nerve network that grows in response to our relationships to others is also the nerve network that enables us to perceive a direct meaningful sense of our own being. Thus *we* are a gift from others. We "become a person through other persons."

This principle is true not only of our human relations; it is fundamentally true in terms of the interdependent origination of all things, impermanence, and the emptiness of any fixed self—all as an expression of inexhaustible non-exclusiveness. This is the divine hologram, the Buddhist dharmadhatu—or the "mind of God"—in which all things embrace and embody each other in an infinite display of reciprocity and nurturance. That is the field out of which we are born. And it is a field that, even within the structure of our life in time, enjoins us to the experience of being fully nurtured and of then being able to fully nurture.

Thus we may see here how this metaphysical principle manifests at the heart of a mental-emotional principle, a social principle, and an ecological principle. This principle was demonstrated to me repeatedly and directly by the experiences of an intrapenetrating totality alive in service to itself in the aspect of all others. And whether it was revealed as the mutual embrace of mirror-like being (as in the chapter titled "Dancing at a Festival") or birth into creation as the function of creative love itself (as in the chapter titled "I and My Father Are One"), our absolute being and our evolutionary drama are the same.

At the mental-emotional level, the immediate recognition of our true mutuality as human beings is compromised by certain primitive hormonal imperatives (which we are technically capable of overriding), by personal and historical trauma, and by the reifications of our separateness in the form of greed, anger, and ignorance. It is also compromised by the mind's acquired categories of physical and social difference, and amplified by fears, family conditioning, cultural history, stories, propaganda, and institutional structure. This, in turn, is exploited by the reactive self-interest of others, and, now, by the destructive and disembodied algorithms of the demonic online matrix, which amplify our delusive conceits. This profound social illness, and all of its consequences, is made possible in the moment of our development that we abandon the immediacy and direct experience of our empathy circuits for the virtual constructs of our programmable mental circuitry. On the other hand, when we are able to rest in the open field of empathetic relationship, no internal conditioning or external propaganda will turn us from our immediate shared presence with others. Propaganda has no place to fall.

This open field also characterizes our primordial relationship to the natural world, a luminous field of reciprocity that our human consciousness once participated in. What was made clear to me in all my experiences was that all creation is woven of one conscious fiber, or reality. That fiber is a mutually interpenetrating totality. When in my last recorded experience I witnessed, and entered into, the creation of worlds, there was no separation between my soul and the world soul; it was one creation in which consciousness was at play, and born of the same love. Put simply, the Earth is luminous truth and reflects back to us the truth that is also our own being.* Hence it is also a field of mutual presence and respect. And it speaks in a language of being that suspends the verbal representations of our thinking mind.

The empathy field, and the natural recognition of mutuality and indebtedness that was once true of our indigenous relationship to the Earth, has been lost to the progressive self-centered cultural, technological, and mental structures that at first distance us from—and then manically and depressively compensate for the loss of—our indigenous connection to the land and to the life of all species, even as we go on destroying. Our capacity for objectification propels our technology, but it has proceeded apart from any reciprocity with the Earth, or, for that matter, with the heart. When we as humans hold to our notion of separation, superiority, or that we alone are truly living or conscious, we confine ourselves to a very small world; and we are dangerous to the network of living beings. Or, as I wrote in a very relevant chapter of a previous book, "No matter how much mastery I gain, if I've not learned the principle of reciprocity, I'm out on a limb."†

The point is that the dysfunctions, disharmonies, and disasters that we experience or enable, both in our personal, social, and ecological lives, and in the lives of our civilizations, are based on that same obscu-

---

*In this regard, see also the dream/vision recorded in my book *Moonlight Leaning Against an Old Rail Fence,* 153–4.
†See, again, *Moonlight Leaning Against an Old Rail Fence,* 220.

ration of the reciprocal field of consciousness. Our separative mode of consciousness is naturally come by, but dysfunctionally entrenched, and often addictively defended. It has its own limited operational value, but it sunders the web of human community and plunders the web of life. And it cannot restore the intrinsic joy of our true being.

Genesis

I said "heart,"
and the heart gathered like a galaxy
at the center of life.

I said "earth," and the heart was encompassed

in a great womb of infinite fecundity,
dark and echoing with unseen presence.

I said tree. And stone.

And with the speaking each emerged
out of the womb of the earth,
which was my body.

I was the body of all.

And when I said
"deer"
there was a leaping,

and it was a leaping that tickled the earth,
and tickled my body,

and space gave way for forests;
and mountains arose
for the deer to bound on.

And I said crow,
and frog,

and raspberries—
I said fruits and thorns—

and my body made room for them all.

With each word, my body shifted
to allow the shape and energies of life.

It sighed and released.
It loved and it let go.

And as it sat up straighter to accommodate,
the bones and organs stretched wider—

till the sky became my breath,
and the sunset became the first smile,
and the sunrise became
the first laughter.

Keep the Energy Circulating

*W*e are energetic beings in an energetic universe manifesting here and there as matter. Our own hearts send out electromagnetic waves into the environment and throughout the body; electrical ions charge and circulate through our neural network; all our protoplasm is in a colloidal dance. The "body" doesn't *breathe* so much as *it is breathed* by the reciprocal and rhythmic functions of life. The right imaging would reveal our cellular network as a community of dancing flames. The free flow of energy and information, within and beyond our fluid and dancing inner sea of neuropeptide transmitters and cellular responders, governed by an energetic field of self-organizing integrity and reciprocity, is the basis of health and happiness.

The electromagnetic fields that take the shape known as a *torus* are seen to surround all alive energetic systems—whether galaxies, the solar system, the Earth, the body, the heart, or a single cell. These fields are open and interactive, coherent and harmonic, self-organizing, and perhaps one holographic reality. Thus they are integrative of the body, and integrative of the body with the wider fields of energy and information around it. Therefore, while a seemingly material expression, the body may be experienced inwardly as fully and joyfully coherent with, and transparent to, the greater dimensions of being.

However, when our subjective representations of experience typically become overwhelmed, we retreat from the threatening realms of vulnerability and reciprocity; that is, from our openness to the dance.

We contract and congeal, in our psyches and in our protoplasm. We congeal the flow of life to fixed representations, identifications, and points of view; and we congeal the flow of bodily and emotional energy, in turn. We are contracted in our awareness, in our feeling life, and in our behaviors. This leaves us off-center in our response to life.

We try to live as if we could disconnect from the full field of being; and we deepen, or reinforce, both our subjective experience, and our strategy, of disconnection. All of this is made to appear rational, justifiable, and inevitable. But it is, essentially, a dysfunction.

It is important to understand this, and to consciously reverse this logic. Healing can never come from a fixed or a defensive position, but only from surrendering back into the "vulnerability" of the flow of energy; never from our imagined and held separateness, but only from the natural reciprocity and exchange of the energetic field. As Charles Berner, creator of the Enlightenment Intensive, once aptly put it, in essence: whenever we have to make a healing choice, choose in the direction that increases *connection*. This may be first of all in our emotional availability—to God, to others, and to the Universe. But it is also enacted, as circumstances demand, as behaviors that help to restore vulnerability and reciprocity—such as relaxing our avoidance or defensive insularity, reaching out, and practicing authentic communication.

Consciously working with the therapeutic processes of our emotional recovery work; with the reciprocal field of the heart (such as in *tonglen*, which we will touch on later); or with the energetic flow of the breath, the body, and the awareness together (as in various yogic and qigong practices) can help to restore the field of compassion, reciprocity, integration, and healing.

Life is energy and presence. The physical body is the outer form, or display, of our essential energy and presence. In our normal externalized mode of perception, we image and see the body in its aspect of a physical four-limbed form, with a complex inside, interacting with the world. When our external perceptions and projections relax, and we rest in the non-dual immediacy and introspection of contemplative aware-ness, our true body is apprehended as the body of presence; and that presence includes the whole display of body and world, an inexhaustible non-exclusiveness.

The nature of being, and the nature of awareness itself, is fluid, luminous, and transparent. It has no inherent "sticking points" or obscuration. And the individuality that arises as the body, an extension of both the aware and the energetic aspect of being, is also inherently fluid, transparent, and unobstructed. Thus, coherence and transparency extend to our physical embodiment as well. And as the mind directs itself, through practice, to become coherent—or at one with the body—the body itself becomes the window to transparent being.

Traditional Chinese medicine views mind, energy, and body as one continuum. And it characterizes health as energy flowing freely and naturally, and illness as energy blocked or disrupted in its course. However, just as the processes of mind and ego seem to create many sticking points and obscurations in our awareness, these in turn con-tribute to fixations and incoherence in our bodily function. We are wired such that it is natural for the ego/mind to accumulate a story about the world that is separative and dualistic, based on pleasure and pain, approach and avoidance. This story makes use of the raw materi-als of the body's processes of adjustment to the world, and the body's physical experience of stress or insult. And the story, in turn, frequently prejudices and restricts the body's (and the heart's) natural processes of balance, reintegration, relaxation, and resolution. Consequently, the body acquires fixations and imbalances in function that cause it to lose coherence with the fluid and transparent energetic or etheric grid out of which it arises. The body becomes part of our story. It holds, solidifies, and dramatizes a separative story—or pattern of imbalance—of its own.

Ancient Taoist philosophy evolved a very sophisticated understand-ing of this whole process. It describes how the inherent transparent and creative nature of the Tao ("Early Heaven," it is sometimes called) manifests through the dance of creative energies as the created world of form ("Late Heaven"), and is thus still inherently fluid, creative, coherent, and transparent. Late Heaven might ideally be characterized by the dynamic activity of human life that is in harmony with both heaven and earth. To cultivate and to experience that connection and that harmony with heaven and earth is considered a treasure of human existence. But the reactive feedback loops and misinterpretations of the mind that arise from processing the dualistic experience of form lead to all the patterns of imbalance and contraction that result in physical, emotional, and spiritual illness. That is, we lose track of Heaven. Hence, in the naturalistic Taoist understanding, both physical and spiritual imbalance and, likewise, spiritual and physical healing, are part and parcel of each other.

Our unbalanced behaviors, stemming from our misguided perceptions and interpretations, take us out of harmony and into a world of stunted possibility. The natural coherence of body and breath with the energetic matrix that surrounds and infuses the body becomes disjointed and incoherent insofar as the body and breath now take their cue from feedback loops connected to a disjointed and idiosyncratic story. It is as if the body contracts away from its coherent etheric field and goes its own way, just as the ego contracts from the field of being and seemingly goes its own way.

Many Eastern traditions speak at length about the esoteric physiology of the body, according to their own models, and build in a body-centered process as a support component. But what is of essential significance here is that the body, the psyche, and the spirit are, in major respects, all reflections of each other.

What we may experience is that the movements of the *body* lose their natural harmony and coherence and tend toward greater rigidity and fragmentation. The *breath* likewise becomes restricted and loses its own nourishing and harmonizing function. The *heart* loses its natural openness to, and coherence with, the congruent wave-fields of being—which would otherwise be experienced as harmony, affirmation, and well-being—and becomes subject to negative emotional messages. This negative messaging creates an incoherence in the rhythmic frequency of the heart's own wave-field, compromising the heart's function of promoting the harmony of the whole body, and seriously compromising its own health as well. (This pattern is recognized by both traditional Chinese medicine and by modern research.) And finally, our *awareness* is distracted from its natural transparent quality as it becomes occupied and identified with the mind's continual thinking and imaging.

The ancient Chinese science of energy flow, harmony, and cultivation— only in the last century termed "qigong"—has long been central to my practice and teaching because I have seen how universally it supports others at any stage of their practice. Though qigong has been expressed and taught in many ways or with many emphases, the focus in my teaching is on coherence and transparency.

My experience is that qigong practice is an opportunity to address the totality of disharmony in our function through an integrated approach that engages the body, mind, heart, breath, and movement in a way that reverses and re-habituates the tendency to disharmony and separation, and that restores our expressive being of coherence and transparency.

First, through both moving and still practices, we cultivate and restore the *coherent* functioning of body, mind, breath, and heart with our dynamic energetic matrix. This eliminates most of the mental and emotional noise and discord in the system, which is a product of disharmony and lack of flow. Then our awareness, and this entire coherent system, absent of interference patterns, becomes naturally *transparent* to the awake, joyful, and infinite nature of being.

I have found that, quite universally, as we enter into the movements of qigong—no matter how rigid or awkward we may be at the start, or how new we may be to its principles—it is as if we have sent a message out into the energetic field that we are ready to be re-attuned and restored to its harmonic flow. Gradually the field begins to activate itself and inform our movements. And gradually, as we surrender the control, rigidity, or awkwardness with which we held our bodies, there is a relaxation into the flow of movement, governed by the energy itself.

As the energy circulates, the places that were congested dissolve back into the stream; and the places that were deficient become nourished and full. The result is that we end up feeling like what some part of us suspected life was supposed to feel like in the first place. And we are restored to a taste of Late Heaven.

Whirling

Whirling with the tai chi sword,
I come to a pause, and tend
to the altar flowers—losing their petals
after two weeks. Gratitude owns
me—to be a servant of the dance, a servant
of flowers before our compassionate
lady. The petals drop around me
as I open the sliding door and offer
them to the falling snow. Falling snow,
falling petals, falling in love with
the dance, the circulating gratitude of
all things passing. It could be the snow
whirling in the dance; the flowers
offering me; my fallen petals scattered
to the wind, to the renewal of white
snow falling everywhere. I sit earlier
with a friend who marvels at the beauty
of the snow, taking nothing for
granted, saying: "Why is snow white?"
Why white! It could have been
khaki or maroon. How lucky we are
to inhabit a world where snow is
white. Where leaves dance, where tears
fall, where water flows, where
the circling dance of the heart
has been going on forever.
Where someone is awake to this.

Stories and States

*T*here is one Ground creative energy—and it belongs to the universe as it belongs to us. We are not other than the "creativity of the universe" expressing itself at a dualistic level of awareness. Our "own" primary creative act is the creation of a separate self and an objectified world. After that, the most creative thing the ego-mind does is the creation of mental/emotional states. One of the strongest pieces of "evidence" that we are not that greater conscious loving presence is that we *experience ourselves* as a *mental state* that feels about as far from that presence as we can imagine. And we appear to ourselves to *be* that state. And yet it is our very Ground presence and energy that enables us to create these states, even as it enables us to create the experience of an objectified world.

This is not to say that "I" create the literal world "out there." Rather, it is to say that the world "out there" is not literal. Not non-existent; just non-literal. Hence the sage Longchenpa says, "What appears never becomes what it seems to be."* And further, "Our thoughts never become what they appear to be." It is an *appearance* of objectivity and separateness—and all our consequent *stories* about reality—created by our projective way of experiencing, even as we creatively "introject" the idea of separate self and presume it to be literal. It is the projection and assigning of literal reality that is the ego mind's creative act. (We can see how this easily extends to any innocent or hurtful belief,

---

*See Longchenpa, *You Are the Eyes of the World*, 36.

opinion, or judgment we may have concerning the world, ourselves, or others.) And yet the "raw material" of this activity is the unified field of conscious being from which we have never separated. That unified field naturally gives rise to creation *as it is*. At the level of our egoic sentient functioning—a lesser aspect of that same creative power—it gives rise to the projection of our virtual reality.

As physical and psycho-neurological organisms we experience an array of sensations in response to external stimuli and our cognitive processing of that stimuli. A chemical tide sweeps the body, generating various cell responses that we experience as emotions. We further generate thoughts and images, and stories about our experience. If we identify with these stories, they construct a reality from our raw experience and from previously stored information that further stimulates cell behaviors, sensations, and body responses. While the chemical basis for emotion has a lifetime of perhaps a minute or two, our stories reify, re-stimulate, and perpetuate them according to our storyline. Thus, this is no longer just the experience of a sensation, or even the attribution of a cause. This is a *state*—a mode of being—governed by the fixations of permanence. We call them states because they fix the state of response of the whole psycho-physical organism as a reality of its own. A *state* is a frozen *story*.

We learn this story-making early on in response to emotional experiences that we are not able to resolve, or from which we are not able to return to a state of presence. Thus, the story, and the state, becomes a holding pattern for unresolved experience, and for uncompleted communication. In other words, it is a holding pattern from a breakdown in essential reciprocity that is being dramatized, and with which we then identify. Its ultimate desire is for a relief of that separation.

To give a simple illustration: if, as a child, I have not been able to communicate that my genuine organic needs are not being met—or, equally likely, if my communication is not able to be received—my emotional behavior (including my emotional state, which is a form of behavior) becomes a dramatization of what I need to say to the world at a primal level that has not been heard. Thus, much of what we may call emotions, even as adults, are not genuine emotional responses to the present, but *dramatizations* of emotional states that are chronically expressed, or newly triggered in the moment. This state—this mode of being—is unrecognized for what it is precisely because it is so total, and so self-reinforcing in its programming of our mind/body reality. It expresses as the "me" I know.

Understand that I am not speaking about unusual pathology here. I'm referring to mechanisms by which much of our everyday experience and behavior is constructed. My thoughts and images will generate sensations and physiological responses that reinforce those thoughts and images, and vice versa. My feelings, my energy states, my physiological responses, are then also forms of behavior that are loyal to what is obliged by the unconscious storyline. For example, if I am upset or irritated, I know very well how to *act* and how to *be* upset or irritated. My *state* program kicks into gear. My body knows how to hold my face, how to hold my body, how to use my voice, how to suppress my awareness or positive life energy, how to dominate my subjective experience, how to appear or act out to others, and so on. It is a complete performance that I take as me. Similarly, if I am tired—a perfectly genuine circumstance—I also know how to *act* tired; I may droop, I may take on an attitude, I may depress my breathing, I may resist whatever I still need to do, I may become less present or more reactive with others. Being tired doesn't require this of me, whereas being in a *state* of tiredness may. The *state* is an ordinary *trance*. If I am tired but *conscious,* however, I can still breathe gently and fully into my body to empower it; I can stay present; I can respond considerately to others, while also responding to my tiredness in whatever way is appropriate.

Conventionally, to be able to integrate my changing states—to have a stable sense of myself as the one moving through these states—is a sign of psychological health. But there is even greater freedom in learning to recognize the manufactured nature of these states in the first place, and of my assumed obligation to them. For then I discover I can choose my behavior and even my energy pattern, rather than being owned by the drama.

Our mental and emotional states are not fixed realities. But they are forms of behavior—modulated by the ego—by which we define our reality. Aside from the unconscious dramatizations of our childhood, the very nature of the ego is to convert the unpredictable spontaneity and responsiveness of being—its essential awakeness, joy, and impermanence—into permanent, predictable, and defensible forms by which we can attribute solidity to a separate self and to the world. As we have said, this is natural—necessitated by, and expressive of, the normal breakdown of intimacy and reciprocity in our human experience. And this breakdown, in turn, is also necessitated by, and expressive of, the prior breakdown of intimacy and reciprocity with the divine life that inhabits us, and which we are.

As if it were not enough that our awareness is already restricted by our chronic mental activity, the creation of states is like a secondary prison wall. But they are only virtual patterns of energy sustained by our *identification*. Disidentifying, we become available again, even through the ups and downs of our day, to experiencing our conscious loving presence.

The Comedian

Dear friend, I would like to exchange my consciousness
with yours—only to find our sand paintings smoothed and erased
by the same sea. Take my hand as we are drawn again
into the same undertow, cast out again onto the same moment,
same gray sky. This body is a wish-fulfilling gem.
I would wish for you to know it just a little. I would like
to hear your laughter in the surf.

It's never new, never old, this gray morning of melting snow,
spring in the tundra, noisy back streets of Istanbul,
paddling home on the Orinoco, picking the dump outside
of Bangalore. This heartache of empty space.
This body temple has no walls. Consciousness burns
through the fat on the frying pan, till all is cast iron, ring
of pure ore. This belly and this brain are warmth rising from
another star. The way the mind arranges things is just an exercise
in creating a world. There's no real truth in it. Imagine:
one thing separate from another, distributed in space—the illusion
of a master set designer! This morning's glimpse behind
the set, how sweet—there's the producer eating a sandwich—
but no need to blow the whistle. The cops shrewdly
mailed out free name tags to all the bank robbers,
who shrewdly decided not to wear them.

Do you find something friendly in all this? So many lives,
one diarist leaving no one out. Go ahead, take an hour. It's Saturday.
You reach for a book of poetry: poems from everywhere—
with the same careful notation, same itch of perception, same

commedia dell'arte *in every heart. I love to read my poetry out loud.*
I want to exchange my consciousness with yours.
I want to tell a joke in every language.
"Poetry," says Jerry Seinfeld, "is bad stand-up comedy."

But we don't need those laugh lines anymore.
The wide open door of the senses is purity itself.

Identification
and Intimacy

*T*he primordial conscious awareness that is alive as the universe, and that embraces all arising experience as one with itself, is the consciousness that is alive as me right now. I am an inherent intimacy with the ground of inexhaustible non-exclusiveness, the essential awake presence out of which all arises. The dualistic, or separative, consciousness that I experience is not in actuality a difference in essence or a difference in consciousness. It is a difference in function: the function of identification.

"Enlightenment" is born into a body with a nervous system. The nervous system has feedback loops like a house of mirrors. Over the course of nervous system mediated experience, we end up in a virtual mirror world that generates its own mirror rules, laws, definitions, habits, identities, motivations, and survival tactics. It circumscribes our awareness—provided we identify with it—within the realm of relative separation, relative un-freedom, and relative un-love. This is the matrix within which our mental activity operates, and from which, having co-opted our essential awake presence, it cannot lead us out.

We are a conscious loving presence that cannot be reduced to a form or a shape; not even to a concept or a structure of consciousness. But what we are has choice, or intention. Our fundamental choice is where to put our attention: on the virtual constructs of the mirror world, or on our *availability* to who we are; on our fixed points of view, or on openness in the present; on our stories that generate or reify our emotional states, or on the primal energy of the felt states themselves; on identification, or on intimacy. What I am is the ability to choose to be simply present as what I am prior to identification—and to notice when I don't. Meditation is a sustained practice in doing that.

Identification is the process by which the mind *reduces* a fluid, spacious, interdependent, and ungraspable reality (our inexhaustible non-exclusiveness) to a set of finite perceptions, ideas, projections, and beliefs, and takes those constructions of the mind for reality itself. Its first function is to assemble primitive, un-self-centered experience into a narrative that becomes introjected as my separate identity, as "me." And its second function is to reduce and reify all subsequent experience into a separate and finite world of perceptions and beliefs consistent with my own separateness.

From the standpoint of ordinary human psychology, this is a necessary and normal function. And the more this constructed self is nurtured with love and the absence of trauma, the more integrated and less fixated the resulting self-narrative and way of looking at the world will be. We may have relative success in our capacity to enjoy life and to relate to others. And, though still naturally identified, we will be less defensive of a separate self, and may be more open to the unknown—even to fields of understanding that allow us to surrender the self into a wider context of being. For in that surrender lies our freedom.

But the *unknown*—the open space before us—is where actual *intimacy* begins, insofar as intimacy lies in our present availability to this moment unmediated by our identification with our own narrative separateness, projections, labels, judgments, and preconceptions. We can only be *identified* with the projections of our own minds. We can only be *intimate* with things as they are, in the absence of those identifications.

I may have a largely comfortable relationship to my everyday experience, which I have a familiar way of representing, or interpreting, to myself. And, of course, equally true, my representations of reality may cause me extreme *discomfort*. In either case, it is still a *representative* reality; and it is only when I surrender all representations, all my projective knowing, that I make myself available to the wider and deeper dimension of my immediate experience, not reduced to my projections or my reactive emotions. This is when I can stay present for my felt states of being without making reality out of them. This is when I can *let you in* such that I can begin to truly recognize *you* and be present for you. This is when I can let in *this moment* in a way that it might have something entirely new to show me.

This is true both for my everyday functional experience and for my times of deep contemplation. Contemplation is pure intimacy practiced for our love of truth; when we open our awareness with naked intention to that which is beyond our projections, and hence unknown and "unborn." It is then, in fact, that I may drop my projections of "absolute" and "relative"—of God and the world—and may discover that each particular moment, and even the emptiness of my own being, or yours, shines with the spacious being of the absolute; and that the absolute is at home here, expressing as *this, now.*

The classic Vedanta teaching from the *Chandogya Upanishad* reads: *Tat Tvam Asi* (or, "That Thou Art"). In other words, it means that the Universal Being, God, or Self, that the mind projects as "out there," is really *our* Being. By egotistical standards the statement is absurd—or dangerous. It would only suggest an inflation of our own ego. But the ego itself is a distortion in perception that projects everything as a version of its own story. In contrast, Tat Tvam Asi suggests an emptying out of the ego's story, and the release of self-aggrandizement and self-centered motivation and identity. The realization *I am that* is a release of my identification with the ego and its mechanisms. I am then in an intimate awareness that is simply open as the eye of an underlying awareness; my presence is only the truth of an underlying Presence; my love is the experience and the expression of an underlying Love; and my *form* is only a play of elements. And nothing else has changed. This book is an affirmation of that reality. And, most importantly, it is an affirmation that *that* reality is ultimately available to our awareness as the truth of what we are.

This returns me to the beautiful image of the primordial Buddha, the "All Good" Samantabhadra, who is referred to in the last chapter of part one titled "I and My Father Are One," as the primordial and universal *aware nature of reality,* and the basis of all awareness. It is *that* awareness that is our awareness; *that* presence that is our presence; *that* love that is our capacity to love. But *He* is inseparable from *Her,* his beloved Samantabhadri—the creative impulse of expression that manifests all appearance, all worlds, to the last iota. She is the aspect of manifestation to his aspect of awareness, and they are one and the same. Together in love they are the sum and substance of all experience and all reality, all that can be known and the knowing of it, in underlying union. (The same understanding is expressed through the images of Shiva and Shakti, or Bhairava and Bhairavi. A Christian contemplative might express a similar awareness in terms of the love dynamic of the Trinity at the heart of all reality.)

That universal power in the form of one androgynous being in the act of loving creation was the subject of my recounted experience in that same chapter, at the end of part one of this book. It was, in a sense, no different from earlier experiences in which I was granted to see from different perspectives. Now I experienced myself as that creative awareness and source participating in created form. I saw that, although I was not other than the loving and creative Awareness that is the Source, when I inevitably *identified* with created appearance, I would equally *identify* as separate self; and Reality—the love union of Samantabhadra and Samantabhadri, or of father, son, and holy spirit—would be sundered into my separated reactive awareness navigating an alien experience, perpetuating disharmony and duality, rather than recognizing it with love. This, then, is the virtual reality maintained by identification.

Intimacy allows me to rest in a relaxed, unconditioned, and unbounded awareness that once again allows me to behold the other, the object of my awareness, as the Beloved—as intimate to my own being, not alien from it. It ultimately restores me to truth. This is not necessarily meant to imply an exotic spiritual state, although it certainly may be a deep contemplative experience. Rather, it is a relaxed and inclusive way of being in the world. It is the mode in which truth may be known and loved in each moment. It is also the mode of self-healing. It can only grow out of my deliberate decision to relax and remain in present awareness and relationship, setting aside the mind's other voices. It is again to become "like a little child," prior to being shocked out of my unmediated experience and open empathy circuits into my mental survival circuits. Its foundation in our practice, we shall see, is *intention* and *openness.*

The Blaze

When you ask, "What is this?"—this cataract
of light that is the world—ask it
from the heart. Allow the naked prayer
of your unknowing to lean like a celebrant
into each occasion of the sense,
never withholding your own death.

What else can you want?

When you see the light in others, let it
strip you of the old skin of your old assumptions.
If you withdraw or turn away,
let it be only in that first moment of their
extraordinary brightness. Then
turn back and pour your soul into that light.

You can circle forever in the self-made shadow
of your own wings, and never behold
how sunlight blazes them with gold.

Intimacy and Healing

*T*he gifts of intimacy and reciprocity coming together with our allowed vulnerability, and enabled by our intention and our openness, is the essential dynamic of our self-healing; and, may it be so, the healing of our communities. This is manifested in our relationship with each other when we practice *genuine communication:* one in which we learn to speak only with the intention of disclosing ourselves to another so that another may *know us;* and when we take responsibility for our own tendency to project, and thus speak without projecting ourselves upon others. And, conversely, this is manifested as we learn to receive others as they genuinely disclose *themselves,* and listen not through the screen of our representations and judgments, but only with the sincere openness and intention to *know who they are.* This simple, but hard to realize, communication is so potent that it is not merely the "precursor" or precondition to our healing work; it is the very essence of healing itself, and healing is already inherent in it.

The almost magical potency of genuine communication comes from the fact that in this simple, forthright, and very human process, we experience—and become the windows of—a great reciprocal reality of being that is continuously self-integrating by its own nature, one that thereby heals and discloses wholeness within and between us, in the midst of our apparent dualities. Or simply put: honesty and empathy, without projection, heal by the very nature of reality. Is this simplest of prescriptions not what we most need at this time? And yet we can easily see, surveying our own behavior and that of others, that this authenticity of communication is a rare capacity that comes at a mature stage of our human development, and even then must be taught and practiced. Our ability to hold the space of this genuine non-projective intimacy and communication with others will largely extend from our capacity to hold it with ourselves. The reestablishment of an open, receptive, and non-projective empathy field with others calls upon, as we have said, the utilization and strengthening of that same "social" neurocircuitry within me that allows me to have an empathic and self-healing relationship with myself.

This self-intimacy entails my capacity and my willingness to disengage from the virtual space of my mental circuitry of representation and judgment, and attune to a listening inwards, an *interoception* of my inner state as it is. Our feeling states, however profound or petty, subtle, pleasant, or painful, are unformed and innocent insofar as, being simply sensations, they have not yet been reified or given form to motivations or identities. Hence, the vulnerability of my inner feeling state—whatever it is—may be said to be the innocent *child* aspect of myself. Whereas, my projective mental circuitry, like a reactive inner parent, may well turn this innocence into my next belief, motivation, behavior, or identity.

But if I turn my attention to rest in my empathy circuits, and simply hold receptive and *accompanying* awareness of my inner state—noticing and opening to the "shape" of the feeling, and where and how it lives in my body and in my felt sense of being—that apparent state may be integrated at a non-reified level of primordial energy and primordial awareness. The integrative consciousness that is able to hold that space may be said to be the maturely nurturing or healing *adult* aspect of myself. And as these two aspects—adult and child—come to rest in a mutual presence, a healing, integration, and resolution may occur, enabling the next moment of growth.

The faculty of interoceptive empathy has natural and intimate access and availability to all of our subjective states, somatic and emotional. But it may be especially called into play as a healing response to our most difficult or painful feelings, or to those that may seem to be most self-negating (although "difficult," "painful," and "self-negating" are not necessarily qualities of the feelings themselves, but of how our minds have learned to respond to them). As we develop our capacity for self-intimacy and self-empathy, we respond by moving *toward* and embracing those feelings in our awareness—not by avoiding, judging, or getting "plugged in."

The following poem, "Go to Her Now," serves as a meditation on this process of healing self-intimacy.

Go to Her Now

Shine the light on your discomfort.
Tune to the fault line
of your distress, and rest
easeful
in the dimension of your least
ease. Stay.

Be steadfast, and sink
as naturally
as water sinks to the root.
Release
all other thoughts.
Embrace
just that sensation
of dis-ease:
the one that speaks to you
about how far you've
traveled
from your bliss;
and gather it to your
heart as
your long-lost child.

Go to her now. Sit
by the river.
Be a faithful mirror and a friend.
You are capable.
You are larger than her.
So hold. Do not deny.
Do not indulge.

Do not collaborate in some new
or old belief, but sit
together in the same light.

Do not just listen to her sad tale,
but listen
to the essence of her tone

until there is
only the feeling and
your love
sounding a common note;
until the ghostly
membrane
of your separation
that surrounds your joy
releases
and reveals its tender
readiness
to be welcomed back
into awareness,
like a child
happy to
be welcomed
back into its mother's
arms.

Do not be intimidated
by the cries
that hide beneath the floorboards
or the eaves.

Go to them now
with love.
Shine the light on your discomfort.
Rest easefully
in the dimension of
your least ease.

There is a greater secret you both share.

Intention and
Openness

*W*hen I had my crisis and my first deep understanding at the age of eighteen, there were two qualities that served me, even in the midst of ego-clinging and mental chaos. They were, first, a genuine intention to know the truth; and, second, an openness to truth as it revealed itself. (Third, we might add, was honesty about what I was observing.) The first two both allow and demand the third. But this honesty is never about *fixed* truth; it is about the truth that will reveal itself and unfold in understanding with continued openness.

In the context of our discursive and reactive mental functioning, where, after all, does the potential for freedom and insight lie? It lies in the two qualities of intention and openness. For these are two qualities that do not in essence reflect the "content" of the mind, but rather reflect a dynamic of existential availability and psychic capacity, or willingness. They allow us to disengage our loyalty to the matrix. Together they are the potential doorway out of identification or conditioning. Thus, they are the foundation of Buddhist meditation—the intention to practice that allows for the open field of *shamata;* the intent openness that allows for the unfolding of *vipashyana* (insight); and the sudden entrance of *prajna* (transcendent realization). They are also the foundation of Christian contemplative prayer ("naked intent upon God"*).

---

*This phrase comes from *The Cloud of Unknowing,* a famous Christian text on contemplation by an anonymous author of the Middle Ages.

And they are the foundation of the True Heart, True Mind Intensive (or Enlightenment Intensive) process that enables similar awakening.

What, then, is intention; and what kind of intention are we talking about? Intention is the orienting direction of the soul, or psyche. It is true that most of what we call intention is driven by the ego's thought system and its relative motivations and representations of its best interest—even if that is to *avoid* the truth of things. However, our deepest *existential* intention is for the truth; and to rest in the truth of our being. (That is, after all, "God's" intention.)

Here we see that intention and openness must become inextricably one. For our existential intention upon the truth is also interdependent with our existential capacity for openness, the *"naked* intention" of *The Cloud of Unknowing.* In the same way, our capacity for openness is interdependent with our intention to experience the truth of things. It is our capacity for such intention that allows us to choose our openness, and our being present, over our conditioned thinking. Intention without such openness is inevitably subject to the ego's motivations. Openness without such intention is potentially open to a wide field of delusion, diversion, or enchantment. It is only our openness that lifts our intention beyond its relative motivations; and our intention that lifts our openness above its relative enchantments. It should perhaps be noted, however, that in those moments when we are vouchsafed the gift of a genuine and selfless love, in which the divine is calling back to us directly, all the aforesaid qualities are already contained within them.

Thus, the true contemplative process (and, in essence, the availability to enlightenment) may be said to actually have three aspects: intention, openness, and an object implied. That is, I'm intent *upon* and open *to* the truth of things. Inasmuch as I am intent upon, and open to, something beyond my knowing, a subtle *inquiry* is implied; not essentially as a verbal formulation, but as a pregnant availability. (This receptive inquiry may be a conscious foundation for one's practice. But there are also occasional instances of spontaneous awakening that may come about because someone's life circumstances, or karmas, have led them to a crisis point of existential inquiry or openness at a subconscious level.)

This openness to "the truth" is an underlying intention that may apply to the whole of things ("what is all this?") or to any of the particularities of the moment. I may find myself open to the truth of God, or to the nature of being. I may be open to the undefined truth of this moment; or open to the truth of who I am or of who you are; or open to the truth of a tree (or any similar word of Scripture). Or I may be genuinely open to the question, "What the hell is going on with me, anyway?" Ultimately, our availability to the truth is *one*. Our intention directs our openness to the object, or focus, of our openness; and our openness keeps our projections—or even our intention—from getting in the way, so that we may be receptively available to the visitations of a new and immediate understanding.

We can also see how the practice of honesty—our availability to, and practice of, the truth—in all the relative affairs of our life is a foundational practice consistent with our intention and availability to all deeper truths. Honesty, without a need to avoid, distort, or project, is an expression of our faith in the nature of what is.

Thus we may check in on ourselves regularly. What is my underlying intention? And what am I open to? And do they correspond? In the Buddha's teaching, it is the clarification of my understanding that leads to the clarification of my intention, and clarification of my intention that leads to the clarification of my behaviors. And such clarification is not a burden, but a support. The mind's reality is indirect and representational; it limits and separates. Intention, openness, and honesty allow us to return to intimacy with original being; and, ultimately, to reveal original ever-present enlightenment that pervades, transcends, and includes the mirror-world of the nervous system. The simple checklist—sincere intention, simple openness, natural honesty—is a helpful and user-friendly reminder, or mantra, to carry with us through the exigencies of the day.

The True Heart, True Mind Intensive retreat that I have referred to is also designed to give sustained support to this very principle within the structured and contemplative container of a dyad communication process. Relational eye contact clarifies and reactivates the fundamental attunement pathways first activated at birth prior to the arising of the ego's stories. We work eye-to-eye, consciousness-to-consciousness, so that we are relating again—with intention, openness, and honesty—to the *being* in others and in ourselves, rather than to mirror images and representations of the mind.

I spend a lot of time in the True Heart, True Mind retreats re-emphasizing the conscious clarification of our intention and openness to the truth as a starting point for every period of contemplation. Each person receives this at his or her own level. One participant some years back, who, in my observation, never quite got the point of the process—and did a lot of talking, but seemingly no contemplation—nevertheless was most enthusiastic about the process at its completion. "And what are you taking away from the process?" I asked. "Well, I really got it that you need intention if you're going to get ahead in life." It wasn't the point of the retreat, but I couldn't disagree. After all, Tsongkhapa says, "Intention is the only creative force in the universe."

As I look back at my own early experience as recorded, I see two corollaries to intention and openness that were also essential to my own growth.

1. Maintain a Fluid Mind: There is a reciprocal dance occurring between our unmediated experience and our instant formation of ideas and concepts. At best, they can support each other, but only if we keep our fluid channels open. What normally happens is that the accumulation of concepts and paradigms of thought begins to harden in us like an atherosclerotic plaque, preventing the fluid movement of thought, awareness, and perception, and resulting in "hardening of the categories." This plaque is also formed as the themes and paradigms of our culture and civilization meld with the reductive conditioning of our own thought processes. This may serve me as an everyday child of my culture, or as a student of past conditioning. But if I wish to remain open to the truth beyond my conditioning, my mind must practice slipping out from under the heavy weight of my assumptions and conditioning, and learn to dance freely again. That may come to look like a growing spaciousness in my thinking, and a more relaxed embrace of paradox, or contradiction. We remind ourselves that our natural capacity for thinking can remain even more rigorous if we "hang loose."

All of this is made easier if one has a mind-training practice—a meditation practice—in which we train the mind to rest in open, nonconceptual awareness, trusting in the open, immediate, and unencumbered dimensions of present-moment experience. This informs our consciousness directly, unmediated by our projections, identifications, and pre-conceived ideas. It gives access to *fields of understanding* beyond the mind's familiar reductions.

2. Recognize the pervasive paradigm and influence of self, or ego: Ego is neither good nor bad. It is a natural process. It doesn't need to be fought with. But we must make a diligent, watchful study of our own self-centeredness, noting honestly in what way it truly contributes to our happiness or freedom; or whether it constrains us within its dynamics of grasping and avoidance, disregard, attachment and loss, fear, searching, separation, and incompleteness—perpetuating the very suffering the ego presumes to defend against. The awareness that is capable of watching the ego dispassionately is the aware self that is capable of ultimately re-experiencing its own wholeness. Again, a meditation practice supports and cultivates our capacity for this.

Buddha Field

Do you know those Buddhist meditations where we see
ourselves as gods or goddesses, or as Buddhas of
the many realms bedecked in silks and jeweled headdresses
and garlanded with flowers, emanating rays of light
to all directions? It is easier with these soft September
afternoons, when the slanting sunlight illumines the pines,
the grasses, the whirling of gnats in the air, with such
a luminous and yielding touch that each thing seems to be
the contented bride of that light; and our physical matter
yields in turn to the searching emptiness of light itself.

Is it not within this perfect equilibrium of temperature
and breeze, when the skin wears like silk, and the surrounding
lull of the crickets drapes like a garland around the relaxed
alchemy of life within and without, that the contrasts
that tell us we are separate individuals subject to the world—
that things are either too "this" or not enough "that"—
dissolve, and there is nothing to indicate that we are not
life itself, and that life is divine? It is easy to catch

on these soft September afternoons an image shimmering
on burnished gold, where, suspended briefly in time,
the fleeting reflects our true felicity, and our Buddha eye
and our Buddha ear sit robed in September, poised
like a cup under the spigot of mysterious bounty.

Transparency
and Coherence

We all probably know what coherence feels like, although we may not always notice, or we may not use that word—for instance, when we're sitting by a stream and are just listening to its sound, or when we feel its gentle rush as if it were in our own bones. For that matter, we feel coherence when we feel our own bones as our own simple structure of place; or feel our center, or the ground beneath us, or the land. We feel coherence when the breath that enters us is also a breath of the land, a breath of the whole body, a rhythm of place.

The heart also knows coherence; when its own electromagnetic field is allowed to rest in, and to set, the resonant tone, the sufficiency of the moment, intrinsically translating a higher coherence into the manifest field of experience. This natural resonance is enabled when our receptive awareness, mediated by the prefrontal cortex, rests without interference or projection, with the way things are; when that resonance arises as a gentle smile, a kind thought, a sense of well being. The breath deepens, sighs, relaxes. We could term this the *heart-brain-breath axis*. We could name it *Presence*. We could even name it *conscious loving presence*. Because the interference patterns, the discordancies of perception, generated by the reptilian-limbic-cortical axis are at peace, there is coherence in both of these axes. There is coherence with something underlying, unified, and present.

There is then, even when consciousness is not fully awakened, a more relaxed access to the unified field out of which experience arises;

there is a greater coherence and availability in our perception, in our emotional state, and in our functioning. This is the first intention, we might say, of all "spiritual" practice. This needn't be a "realized" non-dual consciousness, so to speak. But when our internal warfare stops, when the mind is relaxed and empty, this is in itself a simple and essential non-duality; a coherence of the "dual" and "non-dual" that has nothing to do with definitions or philosophy.

One instruction of sitting Zen is just to "place your mind in your palm." Sitting with my hands resting upright in my lap, left over right, I may struggle to rope in my wandering and incoherent mind; or, I may just invite it to rest in my left palm. This encourages my mind to ground and rest closer to my "center" and offers it a nice warm home.* But how do I place my mind there? Simply by being aware of my palm. Period. No further instruction. No further attainment. No further agenda or ambition. This may seem very restrictive to the mind and the ego. But in fact, if I am able to just rest my mind in my palm, I may come to discover, without trying, that my awareness is open, coherent, and bright. But it is not running after anything. The entire sphere of objective and subjective awareness will become choicelessly available to me—but as the integrative presence of awareness, not as the reactive incoherence of thought. And I may find that there is more delight there—in the palm of my hand—than in the entirety of my mental apparatus.

One Zen poem says, "Silently and serenely, words are forgotten. Vividly and clearly, things appear of themselves."† This is the "silent illumination" of the Chinese Ch'an schools, which would become the *shikan taza,* or "just sitting," of Japanese Zen. Obviously, the mind will

---

*Interestingly, since the hands are so central to our creativity and survival as human beings, it is not surprising that they are inundated with a greater complexity of neural connections to the brain than are most parts of the body. So it may follow that resting our awareness in the palms is especially integrative.

†The poem is "Silent Illumination" by Hung-chih Cheng-chueh. A version of this appears on page 91 in *The Poetry of Enlightenment,* by Ch'an Master Sheng-yen (Dharma Drum Publications, 1987).

not cooperate so easily; but recognizing, returning, and relaxing in the simplicity of this is a great gift.

For a human individual (and, in principle, our species) to navigate the pitfalls and the conditioning of our reactive circuit board and arrive at coherence—even intermittently—is a profound accomplishment, and a gift of deep emotional/spiritual practice. But there is another potential inherent within coherence. And that is the self-awakening of consciousness to the transparent and non-dual wholeness of which it is an expression. We might say it is non-duality awakened to itself, at which point "dual" and "non-dual" lose their meaning. There is simply what is—and We are It, in emptiness and in fullness.

When the obsession with "self" and with "things" is relaxed, all is present as the openness of space, space shining as "things"—not separated into self and other, not separated *from* by a virtual boundary—but empty and lucent, inhabiting us as we inhabit it. That is *transparency,* free of confusion. And it comes of itself.

When, through the teachings, or with the inner promptings of transparency, we apply ourselves to bringing harmony to our confused mind and emotions, and the energies of body and mind relax their conflicting patterns and begin to listen—as with a common ear of knowing—to this moment of presence as it is: that is the *coherence* by which transparency may be received. Our coherence is the optimum ground, or condition, for experiencing our transparency, just as a still lake, unruffled by the wind, is at once transparent to itself, and perfectly transparent to, and reflective of, the moonlight.

On the spiritual path, as in life itself, the *relative* and the *absolute* truth of things, the dual and the non-dual, exist side by side, function together, and are, in fact, one. And the teaching of each may be relevant to different dimensions or stages of our experience and practice. Teachings of direct awakening may do me no good in themselves if I am too confused or too distracted—too incoherent and self-centered—to receive them. I need the practices that return me to coherence: practices of breath and body, of attention and mindfulness, that restore a more integrated presence of being. On the other hand, I may become self-consciously involved with my own "routines of coherence" such that my "mindful" practices become a wholesome "new identity"—a familiar and comforting end in themselves, distracting from the immediacy of a deeper surrender or a direct awakening. (This may invite a different sort of "pinch" from the teacher.) None of this is about "good" or "bad." It is all part of the sustained grace, openness, and balanced maturation of our spiritual practice.

In this regard, Thomas Merton tells a wonderful story in *The Wisdom of the Desert,* accounts of the fourth-century Christian monks of the Egyptian desert. He tells of a monk who goes to the abbot and says, essentially, "As much as I can, I try to be good; I follow all the rules; I say my prayers and practice my meditations. Is there anything else I should do?" And the abbot replies, "Why not be totally turned into fire?"

In truly direct experience, there is no mental contrivance. There is simple transparency to the real. But even within that direct realm of experience there may be sudden quantum shifts in understanding. Buddhism speaks of the *five excellences* of the speaker, the listener, the message, the time, and the place. This reciprocal field is really the mandala of everything! When we become the coherent receiver, that is the time and the place wherein reality can speak itself to us, sometimes in revelation after revelation. Essentially, it is reality in communication with itself.

"All that is has me—universal creativity, pure and total presence—as its root," says one Tibetan text, speaking with the voice of the Absolute. "How things appear is my being. How things arise is my manifestation . . . All that is experienced and your own mind [cannot be other than] the unique primary reality . . . Investigate your mind's real nature so that your pure and total presence may naturally shine forth."*

---

*The source of this quote, *You Are the Eyes of the World,* is a translation of Longchenpa's commentary on a previous text, *The Jewel Ship.* See pages 32–36. Scholar and realized yogi, Longchenpa was and is the supreme embodiment of the Tibetan dzogchen tradition of direct experience. This short volume is perhaps the most concise, complete, and accessible introduction to his radical teaching.

In our deepest contemplation we are advised to surrender our discursive consciousness and our striving self to reality "as it is," inhering in this unnamable space of being the "conceptless deep experience of the fundamental dimension of reality." Longchenpa continues: "Do not make any corrections here . . . Simply stay with that. . . . There is nothing to objectify, seek, or contrive, with body, speech, or mind. . . . Just relax in the reality of this blissful self-generating pristine awareness. . . . This is the activity, in its deepest sense, of the majestic creativity which fashions everything."

When we look at the deepest instructions of Christian contemplation, we find the same instruction, in different terms, to just let Reality be transparent to itself. In the modern contemplative classic, *The Path of Centering Prayer,* the contemplative David Frenette writes, "Let everything be, just as it is, in God."* And, "Learn to let a radiance of God's formless presence, experienced through silence, stillness, and spaciousness, live in you as your prayer." And he quotes Thomas Merton, "And here, where contemplation becomes what it's truly meant to be . . . there is nothing left of any significance but God living in God." That is, there is only the activity, as our same Tibetan text says, "of the majestic creativity that fashions everything."

This is the growing intimacy of Reality transparent to itself, the coherence of God living in God—or the activity of Trinity, the relational nature of God with Himself, in which the contemplative disappears and participates. From this emerges the fullness of a life of a conscious loving presence, in which, our Tibetan text states, "with the compassion which does not arise, does not cease, and is selfless,

---

*I personally consider *The Path of Centering Prayer,* published by Sounds True in 2012, to be a modern contemplative classic of clarity, warmth, and depth, of profound nourishment and value to both beginning and experienced meditators. See pages 94–97. Quoted snippets will never do justice to it. And if a Buddhist contemplative wanted to understand what Christian contemplation is all about, and what is shared in practice, this book of Frenette's is the place to start. Despite any differences in outer language or doctrine, the universal non-dual foundation of all deep contemplative practice and realization becomes clear.

Being-for-others is always available." And David Frenette concurs, "With time, this complete non-self-awareness becomes integrated into the fully alert waking state" and "you become more transparent to the Trinity in more and more of life, empty to God's presence acting through your ordinary activities, more compassionate in your presence to others, more accepting of your own humanity."

Clearly, to find one's own path within the embracing breadth and richness of the great wisdom traditions is an invaluable gift that, optimally, can offer us an infinite container in which to grow in wisdom, in devotion, and in surrender. These various paths of practice are like a rainbow of invitations coming from one Coherent Source that invites us to walk a life path of integrity, compassion, and awakening.

Today our science is also able to see the manifest universe as arising from wave-fields and quantum fluctuations of energy and information. It recognizes a transparent, coherent, holographic, and conscious reality to the whole show. Thus quantum physics offers us another compatible image in the language of science, if we desire one, that sheds light on the import of our spiritual paths, and helps us to understand our relationship to the ground of our being. It refers to the coherent unified field from which all apparent wave-fields, the forces that construct our reality, derive. The full spectrum of electromagnetic fields (including light itself), the gravitational field, and the strong and weak nuclear forces all derive from one coherent field of being that assumes for us here and there the appearance of matter, which is virtually empty space.

This field, quantum theory tells us, was only coherent and unified at the very beginning—in the first milliseconds of intense heat after the "big bang." Immediately it divided to constitute the creative forces of a diverse and seemingly non-coherent reality. However, the other dimension, we are told, in which coherence is realized is in the immeasurably small subatomic distances of measurement. In other words, this primal coherence is not found in another or specific realm, but is *everywhere true* at a measure of discernment finer than that of our everyday reality or even of our most advanced scientific instruments. Can it be that the nature of the unified field is consciousness itself? Or that only the surrendered attunement of consciousness is subtle enough to discern the ever-present unified field?

Even these concepts and principles are transient projections of the mind. The S-matrix theory in quantum physics—echoing the highest teaching of Huayen Buddhism—suggests that there are no selves, things, particles, principles, or even fields in themselves. All is simply an expression of the interpenetrating reality of everything else; the totality, and inconceivable. It is prajnaparamita, beyond all structures of knowing.

On the path, coherence derives from each step of resting consciously with things; resting with body, breath, mind, and heart, just as they are. Eventually our attention may become finer and finer as we drop away, or give away, the identifications and fixations of consciousness at increasingly subtle levels; finer than all outer discernment of form, distance, qualities, and space. Finer than fixations of thought, feeling, judgment, and self-sense. Finer than the distinction between appearance and non-appearance, between being and non-being. Then, breath by breath, and beyond, the motor of awareness and presence hums along with the creative emptiness of being and the spontaneous arising of the moment.

Thus, I may relax and empty out in that *coherence* that is true from the beginning. I open and submit to that *transparency* that is already the case. Subjectively, whatever my path, consciousness enters into the mystery of the Ground; and I discover to my amazement a primordial love-play of relationship that effaces my separate self—even as I am none other than all of this as it is, coherent with the source. This is the naked wakefulness of dharmakaya, alive with compassionate responsiveness; this is God playing and loving within God. Just so, when we practice the compassion meditation of tonglen, or love our neighbor as ourself, or do unto others as we would have them do unto us; these are also acts of coherence, and they are also the expressions of transparency. In all cases, it is my *relaxation* (an easier word for some than *surrender*) that allows Reality to dance with Itself.

clearing

sitting in morning fog,
sun rises by itself

mists dissipate by nature
and emptiness shines through

if i weren't sitting here
i might miss it—

i might still believe in fog

The Path of Practice

❀

When we look at things from the standpoint of our human evolution, we see a species evolving a complex brain circuitry. The scientist and seer Teilhard de Chardin characterized increasing neurological *complexity* as part of a divine evolution allowing for an increasing *interiorization* of consciousness. By "interiorization" he meant essentially that the universe is held within our brains. Although our culture tends to focus on our analytical and conceptual cognitive abilities, extensive spiritual and mystical human testimony makes clear that our brains are also able to directly access more inclusive realms of profound non-dual being and consciousness.

Thus, as a species, our evolution has led to a greater developmental capacity for "revelation." This inherent capacity for a mature unified consciousness is, like many of our developmental capacities, not bestowed as an automatic faculty, but is achieved at the individual human level by a sequential and conscious developmental or evolutionary process within a lifetime—a journey, as we have suggested, characterized by cultivating intention and openness, some manner of sustained contemplative presence, and a growing disidentification from limiting and dualistic mental representations. Our human cultures—like our human psyches—while "over-specialized" and generally reinforcing the status quo, have also been carriers of the resources for transformation.

As with many human faculties, modeling and mentorship are as important as training and practice for nurturing our unfolding abilities. Our wisdom and spiritual practice traditions are the cultural carriers of that direct insight and of the accumulated conscious capacity to offer both modeling and teaching to our humanity on this evolutionary and revelatory journey. In this regard, the traditions and the individual yogi or spiritual adept play a mutually balancing role. Sound traditional wisdom and institutions can keep the individual yogin, or practitioner, from being led astray by the idiosyncrasies of the mind; while profound individual realization will serve to reform, renew, or counterbalance the inevitable human corruptions or limitations of the traditions and their institutions.

Since the conventional culture will not prove the source of enlightened modeling—but more likely of distraction, diversion, and mis-modeling—the wisdom traditions as made manifest through individual teachers, written and oral teachings, and communal support provide an external support system for us individual practitioners. Each tradition has formulated a path of guidance, which, though it may reflect its cultural and historical setting and origin, is intended to point and support the individual to a higher level of integrative understanding.

The Buddha famously claimed not to affirm beliefs, but to teach practice. I believe it is important to recognize that Jesus also came not to teach beliefs, but to teach practice. That is, to teach us to see. To teach us to recognize and to be true to our avataric nature, whether we understand that in a theistic or non-theistic sense.

When we are exposed to ideas relating to a deeper understanding of our human condition, some of us may be content simply to incorporate them into a wider view of life, while others may feel a stronger need to adopt a practical path of transformation, or practice; or to address this question of "How, then, shall I live?" In addition to some of the personal indications I have already shared, I hope it will be useful to briefly describe how two spiritual traditions, Buddhism and Christianity, address the path of practice—with a psychological as well as spiritual depth that is at once deeply mystical and deeply humanistic. I see these both as living traditions, alive beyond their own orthodoxies, streaming from a living source into a transformative future. The same could be said of all the inspired ancient traditions of East and West. And we will see how much we are looking at the same principles of attention, vulnerability, reciprocity, tenderness, disidentification, intention, intimacy, openness, love, contemplative rigor, and true faith as a scientific prescription for the path.

The Path within
the Buddha Dharma

dropping fantasy
in exchange for happiness—
not an easy choice

When I first had my understanding of the nature of the ego—and of my own suffering—I adopted, as I have said, a path of sobriety. I understood that the inner beckonings of the ego were a false solution to my unhappiness, and that they would only return me to being more enmeshed in my own distress. The ego creates pictures for us, as little cocktails of salvation, and it offers them to us as the only solution we know. So it is an act of informed renunciation, an essential asceticism, that allows us initially to say: no, thank you. For me, noticing the ego, but ceasing to identify with its representations as the truth, was key; just as learning to disidentify with alcohol as the truth, more than just intellectual understanding of its role in one's life, is the key to sobriety. There was no room for ambivalence here. I learned to refrain from even that first sip of the ego's reality; and, in succeeding, did not allow myself a shot glass of self-congratulation. This would be extremely hard practice for anyone, except for the fact that, as is said in twelve-step programs, "we came to an understanding" and "we made a decision." There is a very real and scientific support sequence that cannot be bypassed.

After the Buddha's complete and final dissolution of his ego—a surrendered awakening flowing from the intimacy of his sustained contemplative practice—he beheld the field of absolute reality as inherent perfection and joy; and saw clearly, as well, the relative reality of ignorance and causality leading to suffering. At first he despaired of how he might support others in this realization. In the end he formulated his first public talk, the original twelve-step program of recovery from delusive suffering. In it, we can see the applied science and logic of Buddhist wisdom. It gives us a way to look at our own life practice; and, if our recovery is limited, we can ask: Which step am I missing?

THE FOUR NOBLE TRUTHS

The first four steps were known as the Four Noble Truths—*noble* meaning conducive to true understanding, or expressive of awakening. The first was, famously, the truth of suffering, or *dukkha*. This does not actually mean that life itself is inherently suffering or always suffering. Rather, it means that life is characterized by suffering; and that our suffering must be looked into, understood, and addressed. It is easy to take the Buddha's four truths as dictums about how things are. "Life is suffering" or "suffering comes from desire" can simply become beliefs about reality. But the four truths are not doctrines; they are actually indications for a *path* of healing that entails recognition, tending, and realization.

So the *first step* is to recognize our suffering. If our egos were iron bricks, they would be not easily wounded. But the ego is a virtual creation, a vulnerable hypothesis about what I am and how to be an individual—how to live, survive, thrive, and be okay. Our limiting structures of thought, emotion, and behavior are the ego's learned responses and attempted solutions to perceived separation, limitation, and vulnerability; and to the early and subsequent woundings of its self-ideal—which, to maintain the myth of its wholeness, it must deny. Hence, we may be aware of painful feelings, but not of our primary pain; of our relative suffering, but not of our primary suffering. In the absence of insight, it is difficult for us to take healing responsibility even for our immediate vexations or wounded feelings, for we tend to be lost in our perseverating stories about them, and our projections of attribution or blame.

The ego is itself a natural, necessary, and functional development. But if we do not understand the relativity of its structure and function, that ignorance will be the limit of our capacity to realize wholeness or happiness. Thus the *second truth* will tell us that the suffering is due to ignorance about the nature of our own egos—our identification with an inevitably fragmented, incomplete, and needy image of ourselves that believes it can restore itself to happiness and wholeness by craving and grasping after what it projects as desirable, and avoiding or hating what it rejects as undesirable. Because that cycle is based on a fictitious idea of ourselves and of our projections, and on ignorance of our inherent wholeness, it will always leave us suffering from what we can't have or from the loss of what we momentarily do have—and identifying our well-being with the gains and losses. These gains and losses include what C. G. Jung referred to as "our legitimate suffering"—pain, loss, illness, separation, old age, death—and "our neurotic suffering"—the dysfunctional thinking and behavior we adopt as a way to avoid feeling and healing our legitimate pain. The ego is caught in the cycle of trying to manage something that is unmanageable, and that reinforces our separateness.

If we look at the etymology of the Buddhist term dukkha, the word can translate as "difficult to bear," "hard to face into," or "difficult to stand." The original Latin *sufferre* also means "to bear" or "endure." And the Greek etymology of *euphoric* and *dysphoric* originally signifies, as well, a state of mind/body health in which we "bear up" (*phero*)—"well" (*eu*) or "poorly" (*dys*). In the Sanskrit, *su* and *du* are good and bad. And *kha*, a word which sometimes refers to the ethers, or the emptiness of the cosmos, is traced by one scholar to the early Aryan term for "a hole," specifically an *axle hole*. A good axle hole (*su-kha*) is one that is right on center. A bad axle hole (*du-kha*) is one that is off-center, and hence will give a very bumpy, difficult to bear, ride. The ego construct is a very off-centered axle hole for the wheel of life. Trying to make life conform to the ego at the center will lead to a very bumpy ride. Whereas when, in our emptiness, we come to our true center (what, in Ezra Pound's translation, Confucius calls "the unwobbling pivot"*), we experience that the *wholeness of being* itself is at the center—which leads to a smoother ride.

As creatures of wholeness—"all perfect from the beginning," says Buddha; "whole as your father in heaven is whole," says Jesus—the ego, although a virtual formulation of a self, naturally wants to reestablish and express our nature and capacity as intrinsic wholeness or perfection. But it is able to do so only according to its learned and projected images. Hence, we are left grasping and resisting in a world of relative images, reifications, and reductions of reality that can sometimes palliate, but never truly address the heart of, or put an end to, our suffering. Rather, the ego sustains our suffering. It is our off-centered ride on a bumpy chariot.

The *third truth* offers the good news that it doesn't have to be this way. Relatively speaking, because there is a cause, there is a remedy. Our ground nature, our wholeness, is available to us. Suffering is not about the fact that life can be hard. It is about our own seeds of pain that we unwittingly water, that sprout and grow in the absence of knowing how to mindfully and heartfully tend our own garden. Tending begins with the switch from identification to intimacy, from "facing away from" to "facing into"—when, suspending projections (identification), we are able to bring mindful and heartful presence (intimacy) to feelings, acknowledging and staying present for the suffering itself. This enables us to bring our deeper nature as wisdom, compassion, and realization to the cycle of suffering, rather than fueling it with our ignorance.

Thus, the transcendence of this cycle of ignorance, false identification, and suffering is possible. But it will require of us a cultivation of mindfulness and heartfulness that reawakens our experience of—and which are themselves expressions of—our underlying nature as spacious awareness and responsiveness. Easing us from our attachment to compulsive, reified, and fixated ways of perceiving ourselves and the world, we begin to take heart that the spacious reality of impermanence,

---

*See, for example, *Confucius: The Unwobbling Pivot/The Great Digest/The Analects* by Ezra Pound, published by New Directions.

non-fixity, interdependence, and inexhaustible non-exclusiveness—or, we might say, simply, *spacious awareness and loving responsiveness*—is the generous wholeness out of which we arise. When the cycle of refueling our suffering has been put to an end, that is nirvana.

And the *fourth truth* tells us that this release from suffering, and the realization of wholeness, is not going to happen randomly, or while continuing to indulge our current way of thinking. The path of liberation requires a logical and disciplined sequence of steps that enable the transformation of our operating system from dysfunctional to functional, from ignorant to enlightened, and from "dysphoric" to "euphoric." Again, this path is not a doctrine; it is a way.

THE NOBLE EIGHTFOLD PATH

The Buddha elaborated these steps toward enlightenment as the Noble Eightfold Path. The first of these eight steps was "right understanding"— *right* meaning conducive to wholeness. This right understanding is, essentially, right understanding of the four earlier stated truths. For me, this corrective understanding was that the representations of the ego were not going to "get me there." For an alcoholic, it is the understanding that alcohol is not going to "get her there." Prior to that, our intention may be for the next drink or the next ego fix. But when we come to understand, our intentions may change accordingly. That is when we can make a new decision. Thus, the second step of the path is right thinking, or right intention.

We know how easy it is for our right intentions to be undermined. Most often they are undermined not by others, but by our own inner voices and our own unconscious habit patterns. So we must become mindful of our whole life in terms of how it serves to support or to undermine our intentions. This is the equivalent of the "moral inventory." The next three points are regarded as the heart of the ethical teaching. And ethics are primary to our practice. For they express, embody, and reinforce our understanding of others as not separate from ourselves, and affirm that our innate moral recognition is not other than our enlightened recognition. And that to honor in every way the welfare of others is to honor the truth of our own souls. However, we may also see each of these next three steps as part of that same logical link in our practice whereby we become mindful of what habits undermine our intentions, and what habits reinforce them.

The third point, then, is right speech. Traditionally, this is seen in how we conduct ourselves with others—to speak in a way that is both honest and supportive, and to refrain from the ego's negative habits of lying, backbiting, gossip, or hate speech. But equally significant, in this regard, is how we talk to ourselves. Does our self-talk encourage and enable—or inadvertently undermine, distract, or discourage—our own stated intentions? When our intentions are still less than fully conscious and clear, and our self-talk is also less than conscious and clear, this is a perfect recipe for going around in circles. Staying mindful of our self-talk is especially important, because, inasmuch as it consists of the inner promptings and suggestions of our own minds, it is easy to identify with it and to overlook it. We largely exist in this automatic and semi-conscious realm, undermining our own intentions, feeling down, or complaining that we are not really getting anywhere. But when we continually renew our conscious attention to the steps, we are empowered once again.

Vajrayana Buddhism often refers to the three doorways, or functional human realms, of body, speech, and mind. I used to be curious that such equal attention was paid to speech. But this became clear to me as I realized that Buddhism recognizes speech as energy, or expression. And all that we put out energetically, all that radiates from us, is also our speech. So we may ask, "What am I putting out there?" And does it support my—and others'—path to wholeness?

The fourth step is right action. And this can include the full gamut of supportive behavior in our lives—including all the other steps of our contemporary twelve-step recovery programs, or any other indicated paths of growth, healing, and mental, emotional, and spiritual maturity. Again, the term "right" doesn't refer to a moralistic notion, but to one of efficacy.

What is conducive to wholeness? Which of our behaviors are conducive to the wholeness we seek, and which ones undermine it? My right action includes not only my mindful and ethical behavior in my life with others, but also my actions with regard to personal practice, discipline, and faithfulness to all these eight steps. Addressing our neurotic behaviors, cultivating what Buddhism calls "wholesome states of being," acting with support, compassion, and generosity toward others, correcting our misunderstandings, meditation—all of these can come under right action. We can see from all this that each of the steps include all of the others. Our right action is an expression, and is also a form, of right speech; even as right speech, or even right intention, is a form of right action.

TAKING REFUGE

I would like to inject here an aspect of right understanding, right intention, and right action that is also a fundamental principal of Buddhist practice—and of all recovery programs, including Christianity. It is "taking refuge," or surrendering to a higher principle. For the profound transformation that we seek, the ego will never pull itself up by its own imaginary bootstraps. Rather, when we acknowledge that the seemingly self-dependent operating system of the ego is flawed, we discover a mindful and prayerful reciprocity with an underlying truth, or wholeness-of-being, to which we must allow "surrender." So we turn our lives over to a higher power than the ego's thought system. In the absence of that acknowledgement and surrender to a "higher power," "higher self," or higher level of functioning, we are, for all our effort, still working against ourselves, or against that wholeness. For, ultimately, we *are* that higher power. The ego's operating system, with which we are currently identified, is a stand-in for who and what we really are.

Traditionally, the "taking of refuge" is the act by which one becomes "officially" a Buddhist. Here, in our "unofficial" Buddhism, we may refer to it as how we become a student of the truth. Traditionally, the first refuge is in the Buddha, the source of the teaching and the continued model and inspiration for our practice. The second refuge is in the Dharma, the body of the Buddhist teachings, and the universal truth to which it refers. The third refuge is in the Sangha, the association of enlightened beings around the Buddha, who also support or enable our practice; or, more commonly, our fellow practitioners with whom we share and support each other's practice.

But there is another subtle, but practical, level of understanding on which we can appreciate and apply this. The word Buddha means "awakened," and the Buddha is our own fundamental nature and capacity as awakeness, or awareness, prior to its identification with the ego and its projections. It is, in fact, our attentive presence and compassion. When I learned to take refuge in my attentive presence, rather than in my ego's plans for me, I was taking refuge in the Buddha. The Dharma is the truth of things, or the way things are. When, in my attentive presence, I allow things to present themselves as what they are, rather than as my own representations or projections, I am taking refuge in the Dharma. When I re-allow my reciprocity, and the mutually supportive intimacy between myself and the way things are, between my awareness and the objects of my awareness, between myself and others, I am taking refuge in the Sangha—the intimate community of being. I sometimes also think of the primordial awakeness of Samantabhadra as the Buddha, and the dancing manifestation of the way things are, Samantabhadri, as the Dharma. And their intimate oneness and harmony as the Sangha. Lover, Beloved, and the Love between them. And we are that. Thus, rather than taking refuge in the striving, the strategies, the judgments, and the attachments of our addicted egos, the refuge prayer might sound something like this:

I take refuge in my own nature, and in the nature of this moment,
   as the Original Light of awake being.
I take refuge in my own nature, and in the nature of this moment,
   as the Complete Manifestation of the way things are.
I take refuge in my own nature, and in the nature of this moment,
   as the Mutually Dependent and Supportive intimacy of all being.

The refuge prayer, like all prayers, is often recited automatically. But I can also recite it slowly and mindfully, as a meditation, hearing the meaning of each phrase, and of each image reflected in it. It gives me a moment to contemplate, to recognize, and to restore myself to the dimensions of wholeness that are true of this moment. I sometimes practice and offer these three refuge exercises:

1. Notice anything. Notice your *awareness* of it. Say: "My awareness is the original light of awake being."
2. Notice anything—an object; an emotion; the day or the world around you. Say: "This thing is the complete manifestation of awake being. It is part and whole of the way things are."
3. Notice anything. Say: "Your being completely supports me in being what I am. And I give you my complete blessing to be what you are."

These moments of recognition and contemplation help to nourish and heal the mind's wound of separation that undermines our participation in the wholeness of being.

THE EIGHTFOLD PATH, CONTINUED

The fifth principle in the Eightfold Path is right livelihood. Again, this is often viewed in its ethical aspect: to earn our living by honest and ethical means, and not to engage in any work that causes harm to others— the land, the animals, other people, other countries—or that profits at their expense. But it is also an opportunity, I believe, to look at our whole lifestyle—how we have arranged our life—and ask where our priorities lie. Have I created a life for myself that supports or that undermines my consciousness, my values, and my practice? Have I left myself no time for deliberate practice; or to truly be there for others, or for myself? Have I created so much stress, or so much distraction, or so much negative messaging, or so much resentment or self-concern in my daily routine, that it becomes a major obstacle to my mindful intentions? What skillful re-examination, and re-prioritizing, and re-adjustments, can I honestly make to restore and to support more presence in my life?

The sixth point on the path is sometimes translated as right effort, or often as right diligence. But perhaps the most serviceable translation is right energy. This even includes right joy, or right devotion. This allows for all the ways that energy might manifest itself in our practice. Let us look at both sides of this, which are effort and enthusiasm.

On one hand, I can have an intellectual right understanding, right intention, or right ideals; but my practice won't do itself without the deliberate application of my own energy, my own effort. In the beginning, it takes effort to pay attention, to concentrate, to return to mindfulness. It takes effort to pause and to think about others or to take an honest self-inventory. It takes effort to choose to sit and stay put in meditation practice every day. It takes effort to keep our minds on track. It takes extra energy added to any system in order to implement change in the system. Fortunately, that underlying and transformative energy is part of our own deeper capacity, and can be called upon, even though it often sleeps within the coziness of our inertia and of the status quo.

So though there may be times when it seems like an effort, that energy is not effort at all. It is our natural dedication, devotion, inspiration, and faith that arises if our understanding is real and direct, and if our intention is grounded. Thus, once we have allowed our own energy to awaken on behalf of our true intention, that energy does not have to manifest as difficult effort. It will arise as energy itself, or joy, or spiritedness. Yet, conversely, even if it arises as joy or as inspiration in the first place, that joy will not sustain itself without continued applied energy, or effort.

As applied to our meditation and mindfulness practices, the marriage of effort and energy may express itself in four stages. (And, need I say, the stages are not always linear.) The first is that of *applied energy*. It is the determined application and investment of effort over and over again. To return to our sitting. To return to our attention. To repetitively bring it back. To hold it in one place. Our intention is key. Sometimes it may feel like a fierce struggle that at moments becomes unexpectedly easier.

The second stage is *sustained energy,* which is reflected in sustained attention. Now the effort of bringing back our attention goes more smoothly, and less effort is required to rest it in one place. The attention is developing a habit that sustains itself. The third stage might be called *activated energy.* The sense of generating, calling in, or applying effort is replaced by a more spontaneous and enthusiastic affirmation of the energy itself. We have awakened it from its sleeping chamber and its resistance, and it is happy to be its own nature as energy—self-activating and passionate—to apply itself to our practice, to our attention, to our life, and to others. And the fourth stage is *joyful energy.* Attention is joyful, practice is joyful, effort is joyful. It is all one again with its essential nature. It is our deeper nature being coherent with itself.

MINDFULNESS AND CONCENTRATION

We can see how the seventh step, right mindfulness, is really present in, and essential to, all the other steps—even as they all support right mindfulness, which is our conscious presence. It takes mindfulness to shine the light on my intentions. It takes mindfulness to shine the light on my speech and on my behaviors. It takes mindfulness to take refuge in my awake nature, in the nature of how things are, and in mutual reciprocity. In doing so we are also strengthening the foundation that supports our mindfulness.

Our mindfulness may start as learning to pay attention, but as it deepens it becomes our growing capacity to hold the whole spectrum of our experience, and all of our moment-to-moment activity, in the light of conscious presence; in consequence, our attention and our intention, our speech and our actions, and our efforts and our lifestyles, are not separate issues, but are held and supported in the growing light of the heart.

I have always found the term "mindfulness" to be misleadingly mental, and that in truth there is no mindfulness without "heartfulness." Thich Nhat Hanh goes so far as to virtually equate mindfulness with bodhicitta, the spirit of awakening heart/mind. And he beautifully expounds at length the seven miracles of mindfulness.*

The first miracle is to be truly and deeply present for things. The second is to truly let in and grasp the presence of the other. The third miracle is the way our sustained attention is able to nourish the other. The fourth is its capacity to heal, and to relieve another's suffering. The fifth is to see more deeply into the nature of things, as in vipashyana or contemplative inquiry. The sixth miracle is our openness to understanding things or to understanding one another. And the seventh miracle of mindfulness is its capacity for transformation. For mindfulness introduces the light of conscious presence into old habits and fixed patterns of being, giving them space to grow and evolve.

We might say that the eighth step on the path, right concentration, is our mindfulness and our effort directed at our capacity for focused attention on behalf of awakening. Mindfulness and concentration support the first ten steps, just as the first ten steps support them, and mindfulness and concentration also support and strengthen each other. While all the other steps are essential to cultivating the wholesome and liberating ground of our life and of our practice, concentration is what builds the power of the attention to release itself from the mind's habitual web. It is building the core set of muscles that enables us to deflect the bullying of the mind.

While strengthening our capacity for concentration can improve our functioning in every area of our lives, it is specifically in our meditative practice that our capacity for concentration will hold open the door for a more integrative level of experience, and for the sudden awakening of an integrative understanding that is wholly beyond the mind. Not everyone will have a formal meditation practice, and one can live an upright life without one. However, though this is not a fixed rule, if we wish to enjoy the full blessings of realization, the deepening of our concentration in a

---

*See *The Miracle of Mindfulness* by Thich Nhat Hanh. A lengthy discussion is on pages 65–67 in Nhat Hanh's *The Heart of the Buddha's Teaching*.

meditative or prayerful contemplation is the most likely catalyst—and the context within which our separative delusions have a chance to melt, and our Buddha-nature has a chance to be fully recognized.

Some meditation practices are intended primarily to strengthen the muscle of the attention itself. We may start, for example, by just watching or counting the breath. That is a powerful exercise in attention, and necessary to build the muscles with which we can rope the wandering mind. It is what we might call an *exclusive,* or narrowly focused, meditation practice. But it needn't become dry. For we may find that even the raw power of exclusive concentration is enhanced when we cultivate and bring in such heart qualities as love, devotion, and compassion, as well as confidence and equanimity.

As attention deepens, opens, and softens, we may naturally open to whole body awareness along with the breath. And we may proceed with an ever more open and *inclusive* quality of meditative awareness, in which we can be present with a relaxed intimacy that is inclusive of both our "inner" and "outer" worlds, arising interdependently, but empty of all separateness or reification. This is an inexhaustible non-exclusiveness of being and emptiness that fully engages our innate love and the fullness of a compassionate heart. We may find ourselves in an infused awareness or contemplation, emptied and turned inside out by the only meditator, Being itself. Form and emptiness, awareness and manifestation, Samantabhadra and Samantabhadri, are one.

For Our Time

God is love, he said. And this is how
to let God be love in you. That
was his message. And its focus didn't wobble.
Confucius said to watch with affection
the way people grow. And Buddha's doorway
opened from the heart of a loving
universe. But Jesus made it plain for our time:
speak truth to power; a child is greater
than an empire; teach only love,
for that is what you are; the kingdom
is spread out across the earth—
and people do not see it.

The Path within
the Jesus Dharma

*T*he Buddha was a reformer in his own way. He rejected the hidebound orthodoxies and social system of the Brahmins. He dismissed caste distinctions and welcomed all people, men and women, to study the teachings, recognizing all as equal in their innate poverty, and in their aspiration to, and capacity for, enlightenment. And he lived in a world that focused more, perhaps, on the cyclical nature of human experience than on the historical or the political.

But the Jews were a people of history. And Jesus still represents to us a "facing down" of the historical order as we still recognize it in the West. That gives him a special relevance to us. He arose among a people living within the ferment of an occupied state, struggling to understand their relationship to their own heritage, which had largely been co-opted by the intercessions of Greek culture; by a brutal, self-serving, and backstabbing quick succession of Hasmonean and Herodian rulers; by a corrupt religious hierarchy and temple system; and by the collaborations of all with Roman imperialism.

Jesus embodied the deep roots of an earthy Jewish and Semitic mysticism. He too overturned the rules of a hidebound religious and social hierarchy, pointing to what was genuine and essential in human experience. He did not offer the revolt of the Hasmoneans, which had only led to another corrupt political cycle. He offered compassion for the downtrodden soul and alienated state of his people, pointing them back to the wholeness of their inner selves, to their direct, personal, and loving relationship to the Divine and to each other, and to the possibility of complete transformation within that divine love. This was in itself sufficient to cause the lame to walk and the blind to see, whatever other powers he may have possessed. And it was in absolute contradiction to the ruling order.

THE LORD'S PRAYER

We have perhaps only a small, yet generous, part of Jesus's teaching—not the volumes that the Buddha's disciples generated. But if, as with the Four Noble Truths and the Noble Eightfold Path, we were to look at the heart of what we first associate with the teachings of Jesus, it would certainly be the extensive Sermon on the Mount, which includes the Beatitudes and the Lord's Prayer. All fresh teachings tend to take on a conventional way of being presented and of being heard (or of being rejected)—but when we allow ourselves to see them again with fresh eyes, we may discover something new about their relevance to us. Let's just spend a moment with them.

Every teaching has its own spiritual poetry. Yet much of Jesus's teaching may be "lost in translation." This is literally so as it travels from Greek to Latin to English, and so on. The Aramaic language of Jesus, like all the Semitic tongues, is rich with overtones of meaning that would not be lost on its hearers. These meanings may be subject to selection by any translator rooted in Greek or Latin culture, linguistics, and metaphysics. Holistic meanings may become reduced. Less patriarchal resonances may become more patriarchal. And all are subject to the maneuverings of those trying to make their own historical, political, moralistic, or ecclesiastical points. That is why I take pleasure, and find balance, in the Aramaic scholarship of Neil Douglas-Klotz, who endeavors to offer variant interpretations of the teachings of Jesus based on the full Aramaic overtones of meaning. This helps to inspire my own appreciation of the teachings.

Whereas the Greek and Platonic philosophy has a somewhat more dualistic view of the world of illusion and the world of truth, and of the inner and the outer, the Aramaic language seems to resonate with a more holistic worldview. There is no hard separation between spiritual, psychological, and emotional worlds; nor between the realities of the outer community or the inner community of the psyche; nor between their processes of healing. This also underscores the injunction to "love your neighbor as you love yourself." And thus, "The kingdom of God is within you" may also be heard as "The kingdom of God is among you."* This is made more explicit in the Gospel of Thomas, in which Jesus declares, "The kingdom of God is everywhere spread out across the earth, but people do not see it." (As we shall see, the word "kingdom" is not, in fact, the purely masculine term that it appears to be.) And the divine is not so separate from our embodied earthly (and earthy) experience. The word spirit (ruach in Hebrew, ruha in Aramaic) also means breath—as well as soul, wind, or whatever moves or animates life. Douglas-Klotz argues that in the holistic sensing of Semitic cultures, these meanings were overlapping, not exclusive. That the breath or spirit of God is also the breath arising within us was a very real and embodied perception or understanding.†

I will not presume to reproduce all of the etymological scholarship by which Douglas-Klotz fleshes out the original meanings. But I will offer a few examples of how the Aramaic may change our hearing of these teachings that are so familiar to us in the conventional English translations. I give so much attention to this here because I believe it bridges the spirit of Jesus's teachings with the other psychological and spiritual perspectives of this book. I owe this section entirely to the work of Douglas-Klotz in his *Prayers of the Cosmos: Reflections on the Original Meaning of Jesus's Words.* And I am referencing here his

---

*Neil Douglas-Klotz correlates the words "within" and "among" on page 2 of *Prayers of the Cosmos,* published in 1990 by HarperCollins. For a longer discussion, see also Douglas-Klotz's *The Hidden Gospel,* published by Quest Books in 1999, page 18.
†See Douglas-Klotz, *Prayers of the Cosmos,* 48. See also Douglas-Klotz, *The Hidden Gospel,* 42.

major sections therein on the Lord's Prayer and the Beatitudes.* His rich and layered etymologically driven translations and interpretations have allowed me to weave my own commentary and make my own poetic choices. Any errors of interpretation are mine.

"Our Father . . ."

Jesus does elsewhere use the Aramaic word for father, *abba,* in a close and intimate way. But here the word is *abwoon,* which incorporates *ab,* but which suggests the mother-father birthing source of the cosmos. In this cosmic birthing process, according to the mystical science of sounds and letters common to Hebrew and Aramaic, *A* is the original Oneness; *bw* is the parturition, a birthing and a flow of blessing from the interior of this Oneness; *oo* is the divine sound of the breath, the spirit, the energy, that carries this blessing into creation; *n* is the vibration of this energy as it touches, manifests, and interpenetrates form. (This already makes me shiver!) The result (try chanting it inwardly) is remarkably similar to the Sanskrit *aum* (om), which encompasses all of creation.

"Our Father, who art in heaven . . ."

In the Aramaic Lord's Prayer, heaven is *d'bwashmaya.* The root *shem* signifies the light, sound, vibration, name, or word that rises and shines within the entire sphere of being. It is the entire universe that makes abwoon knowable. The ending *-aya,* to quote Douglas-Klotz, "shows that this shining includes every center of activity, every place we see, as well as the potential abilities of all things."† In the words of the great Christian mystic, Jacob Boehme: "If man's eyes were but opened he should see God everywhere in his heaven; for heaven stands in the innermost moving everywhere." And, as the Buddha speaks in the Lankavatara Sutra: "Some day each and every (being) will . . . ascend the stages (to Nirvana). But, if they only realized it, they are *already*

---

*For a more in-depth discussion on the Lord's Prayer and the Beatitudes, see Douglas-Klotz, *Prayers of the Cosmos,* 9–42 and 43–76.
†See Douglas-Klotz, *Prayers of the Cosmos,* 14.

in the Tathagatha's Nirvana for, in Noble Wisdom, all things are in Nirvana from the beginning."

"... *hallowed be thy name. / Thy kingdom come* ..."

"Hallowed" suggests keeping a mindful space for that recognition within us; for honoring and attentive care. Thy Kingdom come in Aramaic is *Teytey malkuthakh*. *Malkuthakh* signifies a realm or ruling principle that guides our lives toward wholeness or unity, and also empowers us to step forward. It is a realm of being, or of potency, that can just as easily be regarded as feminine; a kingdom or a queendom. In fact, the Greek translation, *baseleia,* is a feminine word. It takes Latin and English to officially bestow the masculine sense (and to bury its etymological association with *Malkutah,* the ancient feminine realm of the Earth—one which we may *inherit*). *Teytey* is an intimate and mutually desirous way of a lover saying, "Come here."

In this spirit, based entirely on all the various overtones of meaning cited by Douglas-Klotz, I will re-speak the whole prayer in liberal elaboration. Bear in mind that when his disciples asked, "How shall we pray?" Jesus answered, as in all cases, by conveying our essential relationship to the divine, and how we may allow that relationship to reshape our lives. Not to pray by rote, or for show, but to enter into our own souls, our own psyches, and to cultivate the essence and the integrity of our intention and openness to a higher level of understanding and functioning. Jesus didn't say: "Say these words. Take notes. You'll be quizzed in the morning." He said, "Pray like this. In this spirit."

> *Creative and Radiant Source of my being,*
> *Mother-Father, light of life,*
> *fullness of being, shimmering in all and seeking*
> *to find its way through me—*
> *help me to let go of my preoccupations and my forgetfulness,*

and to keep a clear space inside of me
where I may live in attunement with you,
where I may breathe with you one holy breath.
Come and make your passion my own;
and may your counsel rule my life with a true understanding
of unity; of my interdependent and co-creative
relationship with everything; that I may be actively
one with your desire to see all things unfold in harmony;
and that my words and my acts may be
an ever more consistent and ever more capable
expression of your compassion.

Give me what I need this day to grow; and may
each experience be a source of illumination,
and of insight into my own next step within the circle
of my life. Help me to loose the cords
by which I am bound to my secret debts and secret shames,
and by which I bind others to theirs. May these be reciprocally
absorbed and absolved by my own forgiving,
that I may embrace with emptiness my prior state before
the mind's accumulation of guilt and blame,
the frustrated hopes and tangled threads
by which I shut out your compassion and your light.

And don't let surface things delude me,
or seduce me with false appearances; but free me
from what diverts me and holds me back
from my true purpose. For, after all, you are
the fertility of all, and this is your song, sustaining my life
and all things, from one cosmic age to another.
Truly, I affirm this. And out of this ground, may all
my actions grow, and all blessing come.

This is a prayer of remembrance and of recognition, of devotion and of submission, of agency and of mindfulness. It is the Four Noble Truths and the Eightfold Path in one prayer. And it is the gift of a divine psychologist.

THE BEATITUDES

This deep and tender understanding of the human psyche is present throughout Jesus's teaching. And it is made explicit in the Beatitudes, or, if I may borrow from the apt and felicitous designation of Dale Allen Hoffman, the Be-Attitudes.

Much learned and theological commentary exists regarding all these teachings—Hebrew scriptures resonances, eschatological significance, and so on. But for myself, the most personally inspiring understanding comes from looking at the intimate resonances of the Aramaic, and their immediate psychological and spiritual truth. Again, all the Aramaic meanings below are thanks to Douglas-Klotz.

In Aramaic, the word translated as "blessed" (*tubwayhun*) comes from a root which means "that which is suited for its purpose," "perfectly ripe for the occasion,"* or that which is in timing and in tune with a deeper reality. Thus, if we are to be ripe or ready to attune to that divine realm of unity—or even to the next stages of our own growth—the following circumstances or conditions will contribute to that ripeness.

1. "Blessed are the poor in spirit, for theirs is the kingdom of heaven."

"Poor in spirit" is a traditional Aramaic idiom for humble. And genuine humility certainly makes us ripe for growth and for deeper understanding and practice. (Compare with ancient Zen patriarch Seng-ts'an, who said, "The perfect way knows no difficulty for one

---

*See Neil Douglas-Klotz, *Blessings of the Cosmos* (Louisville, Co.: Sounds True, 2006), 20–21.

not stuck on his own opinions.") Curiously, however, the word for poor here—*l'meskenaee*—encompasses the image of a solid home base, or resting point; or of solidly holding fast to something. Poor is implied only by the possibility of its absence. So we might interpret this as *not* making our home in, and not holding fast to, an egotistical point of view. Or as *making our home* in the spirit.*

Neil Douglas-Klotz actually favors "breath" in this translation, giving this beatitude a very Buddhist flavor. As I hear it: "Ripe and in tune are those who make their home in the breath, for they will be available to the underlying wholeness."

In truth, while our thoughts and egoistic projections take us all over, and into past and future, God, or the Kingdom of Heaven, can only be known *right now,* in the present. The spirit rests right here, in the next breath. When we divest ourselves of the wealth of our attitudes, concepts, and projections, and dwell in the poverty of this moment—in the breath, in the spirit—we have entered the vestibule of God.

2. "Blessed are they that mourn, for they shall be comforted."

The word for mourn (*lawile*) also suggests a deep longing for something to happen, or those who are weak from such longing. "Comfort" (*netbayun*) also connotes "a return from wandering," "united inside by love," "feeling an inner continuity," or seeing "the face of what one longs for."† This is also suggestive of the mourner's acknowledgement of dukkha (suffering)—and, as I wrote earlier, the heartful tending of our own garden ("Tending begins with the switch from identification to intimacy, from 'facing away from' to 'facing into'—when, suspending projections (identification), we are able to bring mindful and heartful presence (intimacy) to feelings, acknowledging and staying present for

---

*See also Douglas-Klotz, *The Hidden Gospel,* 41.
†See, for example, Douglas-Klotz, *Prayers of the Cosmos,* 51.

the suffering itself"). And this, in turn, will enable a "feeling of inner continuity," and of being "united inside by love."

3. *"Blessed are the meek, for they shall inherit the earth."*
Where the Aramaic *l'makikhe* finds its way to English as "meek," the Aramaic would say gentle, or humble. But the roots of the word also imply "one who has softened what is hard or rigid within."* Thus, as above, this softening reflects the release and conversion of our rigid identifications into intimacy or presence, and allows us to receive the fruits of life, of relationship, and of the Earth. To turn with tenderness to our own souls allows us to turn with tenderness to others, and to life itself; and to submit or surrender to God—which is also what *l'makikhe* implies.

4. *"Blessed are they who hunger and thirst after righteousness, for they shall be filled."*
Here hunger is our "right intention." Douglas-Klotz says, "Righteousness (*khenuta*) refers to an inner and outer sense of justice, a base upon which things can rest, and the perfection of a natural stability."† This, again, is the "unwobbling pivot," the wholeness of being. To the extent that our "axle hole" is identified with the self's point of view, justice—or the greater balance—is not fully possible; for justice, righteousness, and balance (both social and personal) require us to see past ourselves to the reality of others, and to the situation as a whole. *Nisbhun*, "filled," or "satisfied," also carries the earthy images of "surrounded by fruit," "encircled by birthing," and "embraced by generation."‡

5. *"Blessed are the merciful, for they shall obtain mercy."*
Douglas-Klotz writes that the words merciful (*lamrahmane*) and mercy (*rahme*) both come from a root that "meant 'womb' or an inner motion

*See, for example, Douglas-Klotz, *Prayers of the Cosmos,* 53–54.
†See, for example, Douglas-Klotz, *Prayers of the Cosmos,* 57.
‡See, again, Douglas-Klotz, *Prayers of the Cosmos,* 57.

extending from the center or depths of the body and radiating heat and ardor." (Isn't this the same divine birthing process invoked at the beginning of the Lord's Prayer?) "The root may also mean 'pity,' 'love,' 'compassion,' 'a long drawn breath extending grace . . .'" (And doesn't this also invoke the compassionate Buddhist practice of tonglen, whereby we breathe in another's suffering, and send back love and blessing on the outbreath?) He further writes, "The association of womb and compassion leads to the image of 'birthing mercy.'" And he quotes Meister Eckhart, "We are all meant to be Mothers of God."*

To this we may add again the words of the ancient Tibetan master Tsongkhapa: "Bring to birth . . . the maternal mind of totally positive intentions towards all beings as towards cherished children." And learn to discriminate "between actions which negate the preciousness of others and actions which affirm and judiciously care for others."

6. "Blessed are the pure in heart, for they shall see God."

Pure (*dadkeyn*) in heart refers to those "consistent" in love or sympathy because they have an abundance of purpose, "like a flower blossoming because that is its nature." Heart (*lebhon*) "carries the sense of any center from which life radiates."† "*Nehzun* can be translated as 'see,' but also points to inner vision or contemplation. The old roots evoke the image of a flash of lightning that appears suddenly in the sky," writes Douglas-Klotz. This also evokes the Buddhist Sanskrit term prajna, and the flash of transcendent non-dual insight or wisdom that may suddenly appear in the sky of the mind made empty and still by contemplation.

7. "Blessed are the peacemakers, for they shall be called the children of God."

The makers (*lahwvday*) of peace refers to those "who not only perform an action, but are committed to it," with such earthy images as "tilling

---

*See, for example, Douglas-Klotz, *Prayers of the Cosmos*, 60.
†See, for example, Douglas-Klotz, *Prayers of the Cosmos*, 63.

the ground," bringing forth fruit, and celebrating. It is "that which is done regularly—despite the odds."* Peace (*shlama*) is health, safety, mutual agreement, that which unifies all parties in sympathy. For me, this evokes one of my favorite personal commandments, as I have previously shared: "Persist as love despite all evidence to the contrary." It is the heart of the Jesus message and the Jesus story, and I believe it is also the essential message of the eighth and ninth beatitudes.

8. "Blessed are they who are persecuted for righteousness' sake, for theirs is the kingdom of heaven" and 9. "Blessed are ye, when men shall revile you, and persecute you, and say all manner of evil against you falsely, for my sake."

This is essential final counsel, for after all, "evidence to the contrary" is also abundant, both around and within us. Neither outer society nor the inner conflicting voices of our own psyches are strewing flowers in our path to righteousness and love. Or justice. "Persecuted" (*detrdep*) can also mean "driven, dominated, dislocated, disunited, or moved by scandal or shame."† And obviously, such "persecution" can come from within and without.

I appreciate Douglas-Klotz's final words here: "Jesus does not, however, either commiserate with us or incite us to seek suffering. He places the reactiveness of society within a cosmic context: if you are dislocated for justice, consider your new home to be the planet—or the universe. The boundaries that provide our margin of safety sometimes also insulate us from our next step. 'Consider adversity as an incitement to take another step' seems to be the message of these final Beatitudes."‡

Our new home is also now in him, in God, in the awakened truth of our essential nature, manifesting as our conscious loving presence.

Jesus was a human being talking to his friends, to his disciples, and

---

*See, for example, Douglas-Klotz, *Prayers of the Cosmos,* 66.
†See, for example, Douglas-Klotz, *Prayers of the Cosmos,* 69.
‡See, again, Douglas-Klotz, *Prayers of the Cosmos,* 69.

to common people. I suspect he didn't make short Biblical proclamations of "Blessed are," but engaged people's understanding in intimate ways.

I am imagining Jesus now moving away from the crowds a bit, trying to balance both sides of his mission, and leading his disciples up the gentle slopes beside Galilee—the crowds following and hovering nearby. He has a clear vision and vocation with regard to the deepest and most promising aspect of the teaching that threads its still immature way through the history of his people—and which is still squandered in the dust of ignorance, hypocrisy, and oppression in the lands of its destiny. If people could only be supported in returning to themselves in truth, in regarding others in truth, and surrendering themselves to God in truth . . . he will offer his life for that.

He looks at his disciples, confused and stumbling; the crowds, ardent, but superficial, blowing with the wind; the fires of a fraught Judea burning all around them, as the fires of a fraught America burn around us. And he speaks these words from his heart:

The Sermon on the Mount Reimagined

"My companions, let us take this time to be together and gather our hearts and our understanding. You have all shown great faith in me, and yet you still know so little of what I come to offer you—or of the treasure you harbor within yourselves. And yet this realm of God's richness and God's power is right here, spread out at our feet. Truly it is within each of you and among us all. It is the home given to all of us.

"Yet we struggle so hard to make our home in our possessions, to make our home in our plans, to make our home in our identities. I tell you, these things are passing by, but your home is not in any of them. Your true home is in your soul, and in the spirit, which is as near to you as your next breath. So breathe with me now, and rest here in this moment, for breath by breath this presence will be made known to you.

"It takes great faith not to place your salvation in your 'plans';

great humility not to place your salvation in your ideas of yourself. But becoming poor in this way, you may surrender your fictitious self for your genuine self. You are becoming ripe to receive the greater blessings of Wholeness, which is the nature in which God already holds you. It will never be defined by your ideas, but only experienced directly as you open more deeply into this moment. Do you find this hard, this teaching that should come as a relief?

"Our plans, our possessions, our identities leave us with so many anxieties, trying to hold the dry leaves of ourselves together in a windstorm. Plans often seem to fail us, love often seems to leave us, the heart is left hanging; and we long for that one thing that would make us whole. We may respond over time by making ourselves more rigid, our hearts harder or more protected, our opinions stronger, the self puffed up or beaten down.

"But I say first soften, and allow back in and hold the simple truth of your suffering, your grief—for it is the reverse face of love. Allow back in and hold the preciousness of your own longing, for it is the calling of love. Here, in this holding, your genuine self will be restored to the love that unites you and makes you whole in the cradle of your own tenderness and presence. This gentleness will restore you to intimacy with your experience, to intimacy with the blessing of others, to intimacy with the blessings of the Earth, to intimacy with God. To turn with tenderness to your own souls allows you to turn with tenderness to others, and to receive more of life itself.

"Now, casting away the illusions and projections of the false self, you will begin to restore balance to your soul. And you can then act to restore balance to the world. Because you can see more clearly, without distortion, with a natural compassion; and with a sense of justice that seeks only to restore and uphold the integrity of people and of situations. And you will discern the opportunities for restoring greater reciprocity even with those with whom you are in conflict.

"Friends, this we are being called to. But there is even a greater secret here that is the true nature of this blessing, the true nature

of the ripeness to which you are being called, by which you are being made suited for a higher purpose. For you are becoming the very womb of blessing. As body, heart, and mind become united, and the divine energy of your own soul is no longer contracted and turned inward to a false self-image, that energy naturally radiates as your full feeling attention, as the ardor of your own love that acts to extend grace.

"My dear friends, is this not the moment then, and have you not yourselves become, the very moment of creation itself, when that same grace was birthed from the womb of God, extending into all manifestation, all appearance, all form? Even as God has birthed us, we are birthing God in each moment. We, but not now we, are the center from which life radiates. This is the path of practice and of love that is laid before you, that the priests of this Earth know nothing about, but is as present before you as the Earth itself. And if you become quiet in your souls, consistent in your love, and abundant in your purpose—in your acts, in your prayers, in your meditation—you will till this ground and bring forth its fruit. You will see God before you on this Earth, and in the lifetime of your body.

"Do I make this sound too easy? Do I puff you up with ideals? No, you know better by now what this world offers, and what your own minds offer. Alas, our minds have manifested the order of this world, and the order of this world dominates our minds and dislocates our souls. Our hearts are driven by the evidence to the contrary of all that I have spoken. We will be persecuted by distraction, doubt, hatred, self-negation; and by despair, perhaps, at our own acts and at the acts of others all around us. All will slander this truth, this way, this genuine life that I offer you. For you will hold a mirror to their own greed, power, and self-hatred, and they will not tolerate it. And you who do good, they will accuse you, and stir up the people against you.

"But I say, turn the face of adversity into the face of encouragement, and persist as love despite all evidence to the contrary.

And be exceedingly glad that this frail mask of negation is all the Deceiver can throw at you, when love is already what you are. For your 'I Am' will be even as my 'I Am'; and your wholeness will be my wholeness; and you will love each other as I have loved you. Be glad with me now, for the time is short, and my time most of all. If you do not tend your own souls, who will? And if you are not here for others, what are you on this Earth? And if you do not let the light shine from you right now, where do you think the light will come from?"

Why Didn't Anybody Tell Us?

Why didn't anybody tell us that as
the pillars of the mind were eased away
the cells would shine with light?
How could we have listened, schooled
as we were in the sociology of conquest,
the lesser genetics of survival?
What could it mean to us that the cells
radiate a generosity of being,
an invitation of happiness to the
surrounding world, a perfectly natural
nimbus of divine love?

Imagine the dinner of supreme elegance.
Your design was approved . . . the partnership
concluded . . . it was the evening of your
excellent debut . . . or perhaps you lost everything
and were happy at last. Picture the summer
grapes fulfilling the waiting crystal; moonlight
dancing across the table of artful hors d'oeuvres.
Open and graceful, your body moved with
a confidence of place as other bodies
relaxed in your presence.

It was a good spring for forsythia,
a good fall for spiraea, re-blooming in full
like the hearts of the dancers—eyes sparkling
like water in the moon. These were not
worldly blessings. They were reflections of
the other side of death—death in this moment,
between the wine and the lilies, when the

air thinned to sunlight and the sunlight
was your name falling evenly on both sides
of separation. No place other than here,
the occasion for your resurrection.

Who would believe me that I saw
you lifting the grail of tenderness to your
neighbor's lips through a veil of transparent
crucifixion across the air; resting
patiently in all your simplicity
between the skittle of cups and platters,
the momentary hesitation of the fountain,
the lull and rise of the voices
riding the tail wind of the violin?

Who would believe me that I saw you
submit to the light of your effacement as the air
yields to host the breeze of lilacs in from
the dooryard? That I heard you say, "See me,
touch my body; it is I, your companion,
the celebrant, the deathless one,
rising in the plain song of the cedars,
and in the spiring strains of the blue spruce."

The Reconciliation
of Reality

❀

The gong sounds in the meditation hall. Its round sound is like a pebble dropped into the pond of confusion, rippling out with renewed coherence. The words of the great teachers echo behind us. The cries of confusion and pain echo around us. We who are gathered here echo with both.

Reality begins with this moment of experience. It is here, moment to moment, that we may welcome into our attention the generous reality of our ground of emptiness, complete and all-sustaining—and which we must yet reconcile with the reality of the mind, whose projections, virtual as they are, are powerful enough to sustain this vast structure of suffering, within and around us: *samsara,* endlessly biting its own tail. These structures are all made of the same stuff, all manifestations of the same underlying emptiness. And yet we must be careful here. We cannot deny their reality and their ability to define our experience. This imaginary fault line runs through each of us and through the world we experience.

For all this, Longchenpa tells us, "Things never become what they appear to be." Neither nirvana nor samsara have any substantial reality of their own. All returns to the mystery of the experiencer. And the reconciliation will always be a living process within her. Reality is a constant shimmer between potential and manifestation, between quantum possibility and apparent form. Though there is an apparent fixity based on our conditioned patterns of repetitive choice, consciousness is free each moment to choose differently. The mystery of our freedom arises from the fact that *we are not other* than that process, not merely *subject* or victim to it. Yet the truth is that we do *appear* to be a victim of so much about this world. And even then we are asked to respond not from the further elaboration of projection and reactivity, but from our wisdom and compassion. The reality we wish for can only arise through us.

The reconciliation of reality is the reconciliation of duality in all its aspects: the reconciliation of the relative with the absolute, of our separateness with our wholeness, of ourselves with others, of our individuality with our reciprocity, of our negativity with our affirmation, of the limitations on our loving with our actual capacity *as* love. Within the polar display of confusion and its absence lies the infinite realm of experience and the ways we give expression to that experience. This is what I also like to refer to as the many realms of "Poetry." Such poetry constitutes the experiences and teachings of the wisdom traditions; such poetry also encompasses the teachings of our own daily path of experience and learning.

How shall we live on this Earth, then? We have the potential to live as a shimmer of freedom and responsibility. As a shimmer of beauty, connectedness, and compassionate activity. As the awakening to, and the fulfillment of, life's true nature. And this will carry us through all the individual possibilities of our experiencing and of our choosing. The great spiritual teachings, the "Dharmas," are like many strings of remembrance tied around the fingers of our forgetfulness; they are resources for our practice. All are a reflection of our original nature—which also reflects the true nature of this moment.

Compassion,
Integration,
and Healing

*T*oday we are able to translate our poetic assertions of the spirit into a language of human development relevant to the science and psychology of our times. At the familiar human level, the drama of our still immature development, and ignorance of our true nature, is enacted in all of the neurological, psychological, and emotional functions that we have come to know, and that are elaborated in our literature, philosophy, and psychology. The evolution of our brain and physiology is itself an expression of our underlying potential, and has already clearly provided us the biological potential for the full reawakening of our consciousness. Its realization, however, is not instinctual, but awake and participatory; for realization is a later-stage expression of freedom and consciousness. It demands our own responsibility in activating this stage of our evolutionary potential.

Let us reconsider our assets. We are launched at conception with the pulsing of the electromagnetic field of the heart, which, like all fields, conveys information essential to the harmonious integration of our inner and outer worlds. The innate integrative and relational nature of the heart and its energetic field is welcomed into incarnation by the heart-field of the mother. Our earliest eye contact awakens the growth of the neural circuits that enable the capacity for attunement and empathy, both to and for others and to and for our own inner experience. The prefrontal cortices of our brains mediate our capacity for engaging mindful awareness in the present, our capacity to attune to the heart-fields of ourselves and others, and our ability to make the choice to do so. And they also mediate our very real capacity to open to a higher integrative awareness.

The entire realm of cognitive-emotional relativity and reactivity proceeds from the collective activity of the instinctive, limbic, and neocortical regions of the brain that capture our free attention and circumscribe it—whereas the capacity for free attention itself, non-reactive awareness, and empathic attunement comes from the yet higher and more integrative region of the brain, the prefrontal cortex. These capacities, as well as the fact that the prefrontal cortex is neurally wired into all the other regions of the brain, enable it to serve as "honest broker," integrating a more presence-based reality in the face of the reactive conditioning of the other regions that sustain a more limited and defensive experience of the self. It is the shift to being able to consciously relate from the higher cognitive centers that lifts our functioning to a greater level of integration and resolution of conflict. This shift is a learned and practiced choice that strengthens related neural pathways. Hence, it is a change in cognition that results from, as well as encourages, substantial behavioral and neurological change.

Our non-judgmental awareness and empathic attunement, mediated by the prefrontal cortex, provide the essential basis for our compassion—our selfless caring for the well-being of life. Our compassion enables us to embrace and welcome all sides of our separative or conflictual experience, both within ourselves, and between ourselves and others, with empathy and without judgment; and it enables the non-integrated parts of our experience to "come in from the cold." Thus compassion allows, and is a prerequisite for, integration. Such integration is the foundation of both emotional and physical healing, and of higher contextual understanding. This, then, is the basis for an existential psychology of actualization that accounts for all of the challenges and all of the capacities already built into the structures of our interpersonal neurobiology. And, as it is spoken in Jewish tradition, this makes us partners with God in healing the world.

Tonglen

*W*e are all disposed, by nature, to love. Yet there is something in us that has learned to contract away from experience; to push away from intimacy; to replace presence and compassion with avoidance, judgment, or control; and to separate from others and even from ourselves. I sometimes refer to this as the FLINCH response: Failure to Love Into the Next Conscious Happening. This is not because we are bad or unloving. It is because we do not know how, in that challenging instance, to access or to exercise our capacity to love.

Based on our human life experience, we all have good reason to flinch, and we've each developed our own flinch mechanisms. We flinch not only in our personal lives, but also in the face of our dire human and planetary condition. Our flinching leaves us separate, more diminished, and less capable, when we desire to be—and the world needs us to be—connected, whole, and capable. How do we overcome this tendency?

The ancient Tibetan practice of tonglen teaches us how to transcend our distancing and our separation, welcome what we thought we couldn't handle, and bless ourselves and others with our capacity for loving presence. In my own practice, I have adopted the essential dynamic of tonglen practice, as taught in the Tibetan Buddhist tradition, as a template for all dimensions of compassion, integration, and healing. This is a vital subject about which I will be writing more extensively in the future, but will only touch on here.*

---

*You are also welcome to listen to an eleven-part series of exercises and teachings I have given on tonglen, which is now on my website: thewholehealthcenter.org.

Tonglen means giving and receiving. Traditionally, tonglen is taught primarily as a practice for increasing our capacity for selfless compassion—which is, of course, the highest ideal of Buddhist spirituality. This compassion also represents a genuine reciprocity, as we learn to outgrow our acquired separateness and limitation that keeps us shut down or less available to others and to ourselves, and to our own experience. I have come to appreciate it as the essential "technology" for the complete integration and healing of our human experience.

Thus in tonglen practice as I have been teaching it, we learn to bring attention to those experiences—of life, of others, or of those parts of ourselves—that our instinctive, emotional, and rational centers might regard as uncomfortable, alien, conflicting, threatening, or overwhelming, and might therefore not allow us to embrace with compassion or intimacy.

Tonglen uses the breath to anchor positive imagery and uses the imagery to support the brain's prefrontal capacity to welcome and embrace all experience. This capacity is imaged as resting in the heart, which is seen as the seat of our actual spiritual capacity to receive dualistic or conflictive imagery and process it in the light of a higher contextual wholeness, integration, and love. In tonglen, we proceed counterintuitively to *breathe in* that which we would normally push away. We breathe it not into our bodies as such, and not to take on a greater sense of burden. We envision breathing the difficulty or the suffering into a realm of vastness and healing within and beyond the heart; and from that place we breathe out the healed image and positive emotion back from the heart to the other person—or into the world, or to ourselves—as an act of love, healing, or blessing.

We breathe in, and greet compassionately, even such emotions as our fear or resistance to the process itself. Our compassion and embrace of self becomes the natural foundation for our compassion and embrace of others. Thus we proceed in safe steps that systematically empower us to welcome our experience with a more all-embracing awareness, replacing judgment, separation, fear, and conflict with compassionate intent and empowerment. This cultivated capacity to consciously practice awareness and compassion reflects a higher level of brain functioning in support of integration and healing, both within ourselves and between people.

Sometimes we may also imagine the suffering we breathe in from another as a dark smoke that has a positive scouring or corrosive effect on the crusty layers of self-centeredness that burden our own hearts. As we see this crust being scoured, our hearts become cleansed and free to shine forth with our natural capacity to bless others. These uses of imagery don't exist in a realm of fantasy, but actually represent a new behavioral choice, as well as a new level of cognition, correlating with neural growth activity in the prefrontal cortex. It moves us developmentally beyond the merely reactive programming of the earlier brain centers.

To my mind, the essence of tonglen is to welcome reality and to bless it, moment by moment. This is possible when our reciprocity circuits are wide open, not constricted. To breathe in is to welcome. To breathe out is to bless. This basic gesture, natural to us when we have been released from our chronic flinch mechanisms, also extends quite naturally to the activation of our compassion on behalf of others. Thus, tonglen practice mounts our receptive empathy and our healing compassion on the in and out breath. Yet the essence of tonglen is already present in the truth of our empathic presence. The seeing and receiving of another in conscious loving presence is already the gift of welcome. And it is already the gift of blessing. Tonglen, therefore, is not just a meditation practice or an exercise. It is the cultivation of a way of being.

The tonglen principle of compassion, reconciliation, and integration is potent down to the deepest level of our own existential suffering and duality. And it is enacted and represented differently in the archetypes of the Buddha and of Jesus as their lives became their paths. Neither soft-pedaled the duality and the suffering of the world. Each was dedicated to the reconciling and transformation of duality in our consciousness and in our acts.

Today, our own times and our historical legacies hang heavy on us. It is difficult to entertain any fantasy of ultimate human enlightenment. But neither Jesus nor the Buddha proposed or predicted the elimination of ignorance or the conquest of "evil." Both proposed a path of love and awakening in which the reconciliation of reality becomes clear.

The Twin Principle

*T*he totality of being, we have seen, exists *in-itself,* yet naturally arises *for-others.* In contrast, the hazy blending of these realities through the distorting lens of mind creates the fictitious joint construction *for-itself,* as if there were a *me* that's here for *me.* The dance of these three in varying proportions—whether I rest in the integrity of the *in-itself* and the *for-others,* or focus on the designs of the *for-itself*—creates all possibility and all experience in this world, and all happiness and all pain.

Our egos, we have seen, struggle to become whole in reference to the world around us, the world of separation as we conceive it. Thus, the ego, whatever the appearance, cannot help but be, ultimately, *for itself.* When I am truly at one in my wholeness—no longer defined by the experience of my separateness in reference to everything, but by the experience of my emptiness, or openness, *as* everything—then that wholeness does not exist as "me." It exists *in-itself.* Resting as the *in-itself,* what I am is naturally inclusive. Insofar as I have put to rest the *for-itself,* I have no basis for exclusion. I naturally exist *for others.* This may sound like a remote principle, or a remote accomplishment. But it is wholly natural to us as what we are. It is as natural as a true and selfless smile or as a blade of grass. It as natural as the experience of *presence,* as natural as a relaxed breath, as natural as our interpersonal neurobiology, in which, we have said, our "personhood is the gift of other persons."

This is the twin principle, the unity of the *in-itself* and the

211

for-others. And, for me, the whole Dharma is contained within that phrase. In the "big picture," as we have looked at it, God—the time-less dharmadhatu, Allah, Ein Sof, Creative Emptiness—exists *in Itself,* and by that very same nature flowers as and for others, which is equally its own wholeness of being. And as we ourselves practice in a way that gradually—or spontaneously—allows us to relax our sep-arateness and our compulsive self-reference, we partake again of the wholeness of our origins, a wholeness *in-itself,* which is equally our path of dedication to all being.

The Taoist sage Chuang-tse writes in his paradoxical style, "For a thing to be separated out (from the whole) is for it to become a thing. For it to become a (complete) thing is for it to de-become. Every single thing both becomes and de-becomes. Both processes being to and fro in the unity of mutual interpenetration."* This is equally a revelatory and an evolutionary understanding that wholeness continually arises as separateness and eventually re-discovers itself as the wholeness it always is. To "de-become," to shed our separateness, is the ultimate realization of our completeness, our in-itself. Hence, Chuang-tse writes, "When a thing's nature is developed to the full [and it de-becomes] there is a return to the spiritual power (through which it came into existence)." This is to be whole as our essential nature, or "father in heaven," is whole. This twin principle is expressed in Buddhism as the twin aspects of wisdom and compassion. And how natural is compassion to wisdom? In the happy words of Ursula Le Guin, in her translation of the *Tao Te Ching:* "You can't be indifferent if you're not different."

We grow wise as we learn to see through the outer appearances of duality and separate self which are the foundation of our self-grasping; and we awaken to the deeper reality of *interbeing.* Such awakened wis-dom cannot be an ivory tower, but the very foundation of awakened compassion. The in-itself *is* for-others. And in our life practice we culti-vate them as one. To parallel a saying of Thoreau: Good for wisdom is

---

*See *Chinese Philosophy in Classical Times,* edited by E. R. Hughes.

the exercise of wisdom. And good for compassion is the exercise of compassion. And good for either is the exercise of the other. In this recognition, and in this practice, is the very nature of totality. And we are that.

It is a well-known story that, one generation before Jesus, the great Jewish sage and rabbi, Hillel, was approached by a man who proposed to convert to Judaism if only Hillel could teach him the whole of the Torah (the first five books of the Hebrew Bible) in the time that the man could keep standing on one foot. Unfazed, Hillel responded, "What is hateful to you, do not do to your neighbor. That is the whole Torah; the rest is commentary. Go and learn it."

To my mind, however, Hillel's most cogent teaching is his famous three questions: "If I am not for me, who will be? And if I am not for you, what am I? And if not now, when?" If I do not become coherent with the essential integrity of my being (the in-itself), no outside power will do that for me. And if I do not support the essential integrity of your being (being for-others), then what does it all mean? I am only half-human and half-integrated. And this is the absolute existential demand of this moment, and each moment. For what other moment is there?

And how does Jesus address this same principle? He does so in his designation of the two greatest commandments, "on which hang the law and the prophets." The first is to "love the Lord thy God with all thy heart and with all thy soul and with all thy strength and with all thy mind." And think about it. Who can do that? This is not a call to conventional piety or sentimental belief. This is a call to the unified being of the whole person. The emphasis is not on the "idea" or the "belief" in God or on some form of spiritual correctness. The emphasis is on "*all* thy heart," and "*all* thy soul," and "*all* thy strength," and "*all* thy mind." We are being called first to come into the *wholeness of our being* in relationship to Being itself, as it is expressed in the truth of this moment. This is the in-itself. And the second commandment, or principle, is "like unto it." It is no different. "Thou shalt love your neighbor *as* yourself." Your in-itself *is* for-others.

This is also the heart-essence of the bodhisattva path, and of the "bodhisattva vow" in Mahayana Buddhism:

- However numberless are sentient beings, I vow to liberate them.
- However inexhaustible are desires and vexations, I vow to resolve them.
- However innumerable the Dharma doors, I vow to enter them.
- However unsurpassable and total the Buddha Way, I vow to realize it.

This is a fervent and passionate vow of both wholeness and dedication. Yet it is also very easy to idealize this vow as a form of cosmic Buddhist spiritual heroism. As a young student I had visions of the eternal cosmic crusade of liberation, dragons being slain, dharma doors—whatever they were—flying open like cosmic wormholes into enlightenment. As such, it may remain abstract, or sophomoric, or simply intimidating as the work of picture-book bodhisattvas. Instead, we may look upon this vow as a quiet moment of tenderness, intimacy, and commitment in our present moment of practice, in which the alchemy of our vow—of the twin principles and of the two commandments—is enabled.

In a world as confusing in its demands on us as this one; in a mind as conflicted and divided against itself as ours; in motivation and purpose that struggles to find a basis on which to unify and establish itself, a vow of this sort is not a heroic fantasy about the future. It is not an impossible promise to some watchful keeper of report cards. It is, like prayer, an act of self-integration. It is the gift of true ground on which we can stand. Logically and temporally speaking, perhaps it can never be realized. But it also can never be thwarted. It is, as Whitman might say, the barbaric yawp of the In-Itself sounding across the rooftops of our self-centeredness.

To practice this vow, I do not have to be "perfect" first. Just as I don't have to be a saint in order to pray. And I do not have to neglect the appropriate concern for my own welfare. But first I dare to allow for a moment—with all my heart, my mind, my soul, and my strength—my absolute alignment with, and commitment to, the welfare, happiness, and awakening to spiritual fulfillment, of all beings. And to vow—to profoundly *intend*—that all of my acts, all of my learning, all of my failures, all of my pleasure and my pain, will be on behalf of that, not counter to that. Do I have a problem with such a vow? And, if not, can I truly let in such a vow?

And second, recognizing that it is all of my self-centeredness— my desires, my vexations, my attachment, my mental and emotional reactivity—that limit my capacity to give myself to such a vow, there naturally arises in my mind and heart—not as a hero, but as a sincere and committed person—my intention, my vow, to resolve and release my limiting characteristics and tendencies. Again, if we recognize this as a matter of integrity, as an act of commitment that is an act of self-integration, it will not now sound so foreign to us.

But how will I do this? How do I resolve and release my limiting vexations? By, third, taking every opportunity given me in each situation in my life to learn, and to learn again, how to release my defensive, grasping, fixated, and conditioned being; that is, by learning wisdom which, if it is true wisdom, is also emotional wisdom. These are the dharma doors that present themselves to me in every moment in accordance with my readiness. And I *vow* to walk through them, even if on the millionth try. And as daunting and endless as all of that may appear, as vast or sublime or endless or ultimate as the wholeness of the Buddha Way, or the Jesus Way, or the Tao may appear, I vow to realize it. Why? Because I am that.

The Activity of Love

*A*t each moment I am offered the opportunity to notice the choice point: whether to love or not. Love may not feel so easily embraced. If the state of my reactive emotions disables my capacity for experiencing love—for resting in conscious loving presence—then I learn to first notice and hold the experience of my reactive state in a compassionate awareness that gradually re-allows my loving presence. If I feel so overwhelmed by past pain and unloving tendencies that the choice to love appears to be a fiction, then I must even begin there: by choosing—by learning how—to love *that*. That is the way. The moment, just as it is, with all of its qualities and sensations, is the appropriate moment of unconditional practice. There comes a time, as the outgrowth of all our development up to that point, when the choice to love is not even a choice, but the only natural response. Until then, we must find support for cultivating consciousness of our chronic trance states of reactive emotion and negativity, and for bringing our full feeling attention to our present condition or circumstance.

The activity of love—which is the experience of directing our full feeling-attention into the heart of our present experiencing—reinvests our sense world, as well as our emotional world, with the pleasure and aliveness that transcends the duality of pleasure and pain. Somewhere, there is always a *decision* involved, followed by the exercise of a practical capacity. There is a potential within us to open the heart, a potential that has nothing to do with mood, sensation, story, or reactive emotion. It occurs on an altogether other level of conscious being or spirit—one that is always true of us.

Its practice consists of learning to notice, to allow, and to reaffirm love's pre-existing reality. It is not a heroic work. It is a tender work; although tenderness can be heroic. The apparent separation from love, when not hardened into its defensive forms of arrogance or depression, arises as true grief. I use the term grief not to refer to the dramatization of sadness. The grief sensation, when not dramatized, is the organic readying of the body to face into the winds of change and transformation; into the winds of loss, past and present; into the winds of letting go. True grief is the grease that allows the drill bit of love through into the previously resistant places. True grief—which is linked to true love through humility and surrender—is the sister of true love and true joy.

The joy may be sweet and expansive. But if there is even a subconscious seed of ego on board, then the ego is also being subtly expanded. Hence, pain or distress also has to arise to allow the continual corrective— the continual folding down of the clay to remove all air bubbles—for the surgeon, or the divine potter, to remove the seed.

When that pain arises for myself, I simply turn my attention toward it and become one—allow it into my whole being, just like the bliss— and sit with it, with humility and presence. Then I may inquire, "What is this?"—and open to the nature or source of the pain. It is always the emergence into consciousness of some unintegrated part of my being, or of some core of lack of integrity in my functioning in life. I say this not in a judgmental way, but just to say that I will sense that there is some area in my thought or behavior that is not integrated, not yet congruent with my soul—part of some subtle addictive pattern, perhaps, that I'm holding onto—that may express itself in my behavior, my thinking, or my identity. Usually, some kind of image from my life will come up and then I can say, "Oh, it is that." Some lack of integrity—at the gross level or at the soul level—that I have not been looking at directly or am otherwise colluding with out of attachment. When that image arises, I do not respond by being proactive, reactive, or resistant. I simply open to it and stay present with it, trusting that, with God's help, the correction will be made. Integrity will deepen. And that is also the activity of love.

Being at Home

We human beings work hard to be "at home," yet we tend to suffer from a deep sense of not being at home. When we are at home, we feel directly connected, through our participation, to the cycles of earth and heaven. Our wholeness, our integrity, is not other than the fruit of our reciprocal relationship to the critical forces of our existence. Our indigenous cultures thus maintained a certain direct relationship to home—though it could be traumatically lost. In many ways, the progress of civilization has been the progress of homelessness. And when we are homeless, we tend to expand, move out, and displace others from their homes. When we lose our integrity, we lose our capacity for reciprocity. When we lose our reciprocity, we lose an essential ingredient of our integrity.

Integrity and reciprocity constitute the fulfillment of the integrative and relational nature of our human lives and psychology, and of the integrative and relational nature of our own heart-fields. It is also the nature of the Primordial Self, or God. It is the essential meaning of the Trinitarian understanding of reality that expresses itself in different language and imagery in all spiritual traditions. The Oneness of Integrity and Reciprocity—of the for-itself and the for-others—is the expressive play of the mystery of non-duality. To be truly at home is to be truly at home in both.

Today, in the face of the social, cultural, technological, and psychological momentum of distraction, alienation, and homelessness, we are challenged to the profound inner work of being at home, for the

218

sake of ourselves and for others. Some of us recognize this as a "life-style issue," as we try to prioritize our fundamental commitment to the land, and to community. Deeply and inwardly, however, it is an act of the heart and of the attention on our inner indigenous ground. It is no less than Jesus's two primary commandments. And because so much of our attention, activity, desires, habits, and identity is geared to surviving and making our way in a world of homelessness, it is even a sacrificial act. To take this meditative or prayerful moment to rest again at home in the humble ground of our intention and openness—to taste of the foundational integrity and reciprocity indigenous to our relationship to being, or spirit—is, for this moment, to surrender the learned projections and agendas of the mind, and the ego's separative pretensions, grasping, or resistance it deems necessary to survival.

We can do this. Though it is a non sequitur to the restlessness of our agendas, we can stop and actively give ourselves a moment to establish our direct sense of home with the ground beneath us, with the Earth beneath and around us. There are no shortcuts here; we must take the time, the attention, and the love. We must take the time and attention to reestablish our sense of home in our bodies and in our breath. We must stop and surrender our attention there. We must make our home in our feeling sensations, not to own or to trample, but to walk lightly, to breathe and to trust the landscape. We walk and rest even there where our deepest griefs arise, or our sensations of shame, or our fears of death. We breathe them in and we offer them back. We make our home in the simple capacity of awareness that illumines our experience.

As we expand our capacity to be at home with what is, we relax the mind's mechanisms of separation, denial, and alienation from experience; the mechanisms underpinning our incoherence of body, mind, and emotions; the incoherence of our conscious and unconscious behaviors and recognitions that necessitate our projections and our reactivity. Our compassion invites, as we have said, our unintegrated parts to come in from the cold. And even here, as we deepen the foundations of our integrity, it is not the final accomplishment or achievement of our separate personhood. We will continually lean into the immensity of our experience—pain, shame, vulnerability—that we cannot ourselves contain or master except by moment-to-moment surrendering to a higher relationship (call it a higher self or higher power). It is a surrender to the nature of reciprocity itself, only through which can our integrity ever be complete. This is the integral nature of meditation and prayer. After all, it is not until we experience the primordial Other as our own being that we will truly surrender our separation and fear of otherness or death in all its forms.

Finally, it can be said, we are at home in that *relationship* which is also the very ground of our being.

At the Edge of the Great Marsh

On the late afternoon marsh, a sea of reed grass
trembles in the least breeze.

This is the pregnant hush of a great voice.
This is the language of the slow.

Here in the awake world is a mutual respect.
The grasses and their witness

are of one intelligence.
The mosquitos nod and give safe passage.

We are each of the other.
Only this silent . . . hearing begins.

Only this slow . . . the earth moves.
There is no forbidden door,

yet we do not seek admittance;
we do not bow in entry before the great open.

There is a community as vast and intimate
as space, and we are its lost children.

I have come back to my home
by the great pine at the edge of the great marsh.

Lone spider threads glisten silver in the late sun
like slender streaks of moonlight.

All share one tremulous anticipation as sun paints
the marsh from descending angles,

and the air grows cool: The Great Mother Bear
is coming in her dark robes

to hold close the trembling tribes;
to wear them as her own fur.

To keep them to the world's end.
To be shown through with the new day.

Embodying

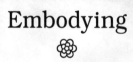

Before we are through, I'd like to offer a few practical indications and sequential meditation exercises that can support us in exercising an open and integrated awareness—integrated, on the one hand, with our physical embodiment, and, on the other, with our transparent being.

As you will note, I put tremendous value on "being the body." Our Western culture has always placed the body (with or without shame) at the low end of the metaphysical spectrum, with "spirit" or "truth" at the other. I'd say that was true if what we termed "body" was the body of our contracted, fixated, and externalized ways of seeing, perpetuated by mind, that separated us from the all-pervading radiance of truth. On the other hand, shorn of dualistic projection, the subjective experience of body is an intimate expression of our being that invites us out of the mind, and that opens onto the wide field of our true presence. This begins as we simply turn our attention from the projections of the mind to our contemplative interoception of the body itself.

There are many ways to sit still and open ourselves to more integrated and surrendered states of awareness. Such simple instructions as "sit down," "breathe," "pay attention," "feel," "be in your body," "rest at your heart," "allow," "begin again," or speaking words of devotion, not only serve us at the very beginning, but also never lose their currency. As the attention acquires some staying power, there are other instructions of the body, mind, and heart that help to refine our attention, our understanding, our communion, and our process of integration. Consciously exercising the attention, the ability to place it, and the ability to sustain it, is fundamental. And so to watch the breath, or to count the breaths, is worthy of extended practice. Alternatively, just to rest the mind in the upturned palm of the hand, or to sit with "choiceless awareness" and let all be as it is, is a profound but often more difficult business amidst the sandstorm of obstructing thought or emotion.

But its simplicity is powerfully integrative over the long term. All of this, of course, may also be linked to the imagery, prayer, devotion, and contemplative insights of the various spiritual traditions, and to offering ourselves into the hands of God.

There is a stage in the practice of "just sitting with open awareness" when awareness actually does become empty and open to things as they are. This is like a mirror that misses nothing, but sticks on nothing. Any discrete mental, emotional, or sense experience may register in awareness—may rise in focus and fade again—but is not grabbed onto or elaborated by the mind. Obviously, this becomes more possible as the thinking mind becomes more calm or stable. Though some sitting practices are intended to throw us into the water of the open field, giving room for our capacity for attention to sink or swim, I find it skillful and kind to offer an inner tube, or swimming lesson, tutoring the wayward and preoccupied mind in gradually embracing and settling into a wide field of awareness.

There is a concise *mantric* reminder that I recommend as a potent ally or summary instruction for when we sit for meditation and the mind is still too distracted to find its purchase. The mantra is "body, breath, and being." First, just turn to the body, the body, the body! "Oh, right," says the attention. It is an exercise instruction that we may need over and over. In other words: drop your mind out of your head. Now! At least we have gravity working for us.

We could begin with the breath, or with resting at the heart, or even with listening. However, I often begin with the body because I find that for many, in the beginning, it offers the lowest or most grounding anchor, or center of gravity, for the spacey mind—far from the head. To feel my backside on my seat doesn't leave me much space to run. This sense of body will eventually generalize to the whole body, and naturally include the breath. So now, as I focus on the breath, it is already anchored in the body. We take as much time as we need, just with the *body,* or just with the *breath,* for them to become "real," and to begin to root the attention. When sufficiently anchored in body and breath, we may enlarge our awareness to include a non-reactive sense of our present state of being. In the beginning, this may most often be the sense of our mental or emotional "feeling" state. In time, we may come to discern, behind these states, the simple sense of our "presence of being" that rests as well in our body, in our breath, and in our hearts.

A more elaborated and more comprehensive version of this process of integrated awareness is offered in the first of three meditation sequences below. These are "Buddhist" meditation exercises inasmuch as they take a non-theistic and phenomenological approach to addressing the experiences of consciousness. Other traditions offer other avenues of entry into the realm of integrated and transparent mind and heart.

You may notice the natural support role that both mantras and/or mudras play in the meditations I describe. So, as a prequel, I would first like to address the use and significance of mantras and mudras in the broadest sense, and their relationship to the mind.

Mantra and Mudra

*M*ind (in the brilliantly apt and precise definition of psychologist Daniel Siegel) is the "relational and embodied process that regulates the flow of energy and information."* (It is a definition worth contemplating.) In short, your mind is *what you are experiencing at this moment.* When we are resting in, or operating with, our underlying capacity for open awareness, our "big mind," "true mind," or "nature of mind" is coherent with, transparent to, and at one with the field of transformation, manifestation, and information ever arising spontaneously as the present moment. To the extent that we are operating, as usual, from our ego-mind, or "small mind," we are regulating the flow of energy and information to support the maintenance of fixed states of being, fixed points of view, fixed patterns of response, and fixed identity.

If we wish to mature and to evolve, we find ourselves in the delicate position of needing to self-correct our own operating system even while in full operation—while fully believing in, conditioned by, even addicted to, that very system. No outside mechanic is going to lift the lid and do it for us. Neither is it about pulling ourselves up by our own bootstraps, which is also the ego's illusory construction. Rather, as we have suggested, there is a delicate balance between aligning with the intention that arises from our deepest evolutionary core and maintaining the openness that relaxes our commitment to, and preoccupation with, our limited conditioning of awareness and behavior. Then we are

---

*See Daniel Siegel, *Mindsight: The New Science of Personal Transformation* (New York, Ny.: Bantam, 2010), 52.

maximally available—which the Beatitudes call "ripeness"—to awakening to that deeper reciprocity with Being, and to our own learning experiences that help us outgrow our projected separateness. We could say: relax the constriction, or the denial, and life does the rest. This same principle of reciprocity has been expressed in the maxim that if we take one step toward God, God will take ten steps toward us. Our part is in how we make ourselves available.

Our capacity to walk this path of availability is diverted or supported—as we have seen with the Eightfold Path—by the nature of our personal and cultural belief systems and assumptions, and by our understanding and our intentions, right down to the level of our habitual *self-talk*. And, equally, by our chronic *attitudes*—how we "hold ourselves" with regard to the world, physically, mentally, and emotionally—which also signals our availability, or its lack, to the reciprocal processes of growth.

Speech is energy and invocation. Words are packets of information. Information is the agent of transformation. In humans, "right speech," right words, and right information is that which is in harmony with the universal and self-organizing principles of integrity and reciprocity. They are conducive to wholeness, and to the "big mind" of wholeness. Right speech, as we have seen, necessitates replacing our habitual round of destructive, negative, or petty self-talk or messaging—as well as our negative interpersonal messaging—with supportive or instructive messaging.

This might also be our broadest definition of the term *mantra*—what we are telling ourselves. "Mantra" translates as corrective practice (*tra*) for the mind (*man*). And mantras, whether they are a charged formulation of words or sounds given by one's spiritual mentor, or simply the precise word or words offered and held at the right time, are supplying necessary energy and information to support the mind's shift or integration of attention. The right words, spoken at the right time to a receptive mind—or in order to induce that receptivity—can play an essential role in directing the mind's attention and availability to deeper levels of integrity and reciprocity; that is, to embodying our spiritual growth and practice. And we may notice the many ways this principle of mantra is naturally incorporated into spiritual teachings, and is a natural part of our meditation and prayer practices.

The second principle of availability referred to above, along with attention to our chronic speech, is attention to our chronic attitudes or positioning. This second instance necessitates awareness of how our conditioning is held in our chronic positions—our mental, emotional, and physical gestures, attitudes, and fixed positions, or postures. This is the broadest definition of the term *mudra*—how we are holding ourselves. "Mudra" means gesture or pose. It also means seal. So we need to be mindful of what positions we are sealing ourselves into.

We have suggested earlier that the body, psyche, and spirit are interactive reflections of each other—ultimately a single field. The physical body is the outer display of our essential energy and presence—and chronic attitudes. We might think of these attitudes as our unconscious psychic mudras. In turn, the gestures and postures of the physical body may either reinforce our conditioned and unconscious states, or consciously invite and support the psyche's availability to a more integrated and reciprocal experience of being. Thus we may appreciate the way in which physical mudras are also incorporated into spiritual and meditation practices—in standing, bowing, kneeling, or even whirling; with palms raised high, offered out, gathered at the heart, or upturned or downturned on our laps; with fingers touching in ways that make certain energetic connections; or in the very grounded, open, and upright postures of most Buddhist meditation.

Along a mountain path I once saw an elderly Buddhist nun who was standing with her bent elbows held high upward and leaning back. I asked her what she was doing. She laughed and said, "You can't be depressed when your armpits are open to the sky."

Seen in this way, we can also appreciate that the meaning and principles of mantra or mudra apply not only to relatively esoteric practices, but also to every moment in our daily lives. I can ask myself at any moment, "What am I telling myself?" And, "What position am I holding?" And, "What do they make me available to or keep me from being available to?"

These meditations offer us an opportunity to *embody* our understanding in our practice, and to embody our practice in a way that opens new windows on our understanding.

Your Left Palm

What if we loved our left palm?
The open space that holds all open space.
The empty cradle of all tenderness.
Look at it now. Is it not your left palm
looking at itself? The circle of your own
completeness? Awake by your side,
is it not the bright companion of
your daily walk? At rest in your lap,
is it not the nest of your simplicity?
Held out to the world, is it not
the beacon of your love?

Comprehensive
Detached Awareness

*T*he end result of the following structured practice of comprehensive detached awareness is identical to the open-ended and naturally comprehensive practice of "silent illumination" in Chinese Ch'an, or "just sitting" (shikan taza) in Japanese Zen, when we may sit with an integrated, but unmotivated, infused, and choiceless awareness of our inner and outer reality. There may come a time when, from practice, the mind naturally turns to that open field. And an exercise that is helpful in the beginning can become superfluous at other times. We can use all these structured meditations as a support in our practice as long as we need them, and whenever we need them—either to lay a strong foundation for our practice, or as an aid to brush the cobwebs systematically from our minds, or as a brief "checklist" to see that we have totally released out attention into the field. The structure of these exercises allows us to build and strengthen the "scaffolding" of our comprehensive awareness step by step. And they will likely serve us in our meditation for a long time to come.

1. Begin by noticing your "body-ness." (I use the suffix "-ness" in this exercise to suggest "the whole realm of.") Include any sensations related to the whole realm of experience of being a body or being in a body. Notice, for instance, the sensation of your backside on the chair or cushion, or your feet on the floor. (I find it helpful to start with a sensation that grounds us in the

lower part of our body.) *Stay with that sensation a while.* You may also notice the sensation of one part of your body resting against another part of your body, or your hands on your lap or resting against each other. *Train your attention to stay present with each sensation, even while including the next.* Notice the inner sensation of the posture you're sitting in, or the shape your body is taking in space. Notice the rise and fall of your body with the breath, or the sensation of breath in your nostrils. Air temperature on your skin. Any sensation in the body that feels comfortable or relaxed. Any sensation that feels tense or uncomfortable. Just let them be one with all other sensations. Gradually, just stay open to noticing and including the entirety of the sensations of the body, just as they are, as one whole sensation, without picking and choosing. Take as much time as you need or want before going on.

2. While continuing to notice your body-ness, also notice your "breathing-ness." Notice the overall awareness of the sensation of the regular rhythm of the breath breathing your body, the regularity of expansion and release. You are a breathing body. Let your awareness of body-ness and of breathing-ness become one awareness. *Take some time.*

3. Now, while continuing to notice and to rest in your body-ness and your breathing-ness, notice as well your "feeling-ness." That includes the *feeling sensation* of any emotion you're aware of, any feeling you "carry in your heart," the sensation of mood and energy level, even the sensation of any attitude you might be carrying—as if they were also bodily sensations. This is trickier because it is natural for stories to arise in connection with our feelings—what it means about me, what's going to happen, who or what is responsible, and so on. Stories are not the feelings. Feel free to drop them for now and just discern the actual feeling sensation. Without attaching labels, judgments, or stories, continue to notice your overall feeling-ness, without avoiding

any feeling sensation or searching for any feeling sensation. Take some time with this. Notice where feeling sensations live in the body. Allow yourself to continue to be aware overall of your body-ness, your breathing-ness, and your feeling-ness as one whole sensation. Notice if it is easier to rest with feelings if they are at one with your body and your breath.

4. Take some time just to notice yourself as a sensing, breathing, feeling body, without needing words to describe it.

5. Now include in your awareness your "hearing-ness." Remain an open antenna for all incoming sounds. Neither grasp nor avoid sounds. Just be an open antenna to the ocean of sound as it rises in your hearing. Sounds will rise and fall, become subtler, get picked up from farther away. Just let them be and let them be one. Even the silence can be heard.

6. Let all of the above continue to be conscious and present, and continue to expand your conscious awareness to include your seeing-ness. Notice your field of vision. (As a rule, open-eyed practice may seem distracting at first, but it is more integrative.) If eyes are closed, just notice the visual field. Notice your *sense* of seeing-ness. If eyes are open, see your field of vision innocently, as if seeing for the first time, without needing to know the names of things or think about what they are. Relax your seeing and let it extend to the periphery of the field. See everything simply as color, shape, contrast, and pattern.

7. Now take some time to be aware of just your seeing-ness and your hearing-ness together as one whole awareness. After a while, continuing to practice this fused awareness, gradually include back into your unified awareness your breathing-ness, your body-ness, and your feeling-ness.

8. As you are here—simply noticing your body-ness, your breathing-ness, your feeling-ness, your hearing-ness, and your seeing-ness— no doubt thoughts are also arising moment to moment. The mind gives rise to thoughts like the world gives rise to sounds.

So just *notice* your own "thinking-ness." Individual thoughts, or sequences of thought, pass by. You needn't give thoughts extra attention nor exclude them. Like sounds, they rise and pass, loud or subtle, associated or discrete. They are just part of the scenery. Allow the thought scenery to be present without judgment. If you judge, just notice it. Notice that judgment is also simply a thought. Rather than being lost in thinking-ness, you may simply notice thinking-ness, while continuing to keep your whole awareness open to your body-ness, your breathing-ness, your feeling-ness, your hearing-ness, and your seeing-ness. Thinking loses its dominant power when it has to share the stage with present moment awareness. Remain aware of it all as one whole awareness.

9. Notice awareness itself—the awareness that makes *knowing* possible. Notice the *quality* or *capacity* of awareness, your ability to be aware. Notice that you are *aware* of your *awareness;* that you can *notice* your *noticing.* Notice this *fact of awareness* as distinct from all these things that have been arising *in your awareness* up to now. Notice that thoughts, sounds, feelings, and sensations come and go. They come and go in your awareness. Your awareness continues. Continue to be aware of the sense of your awareness, your awareness that is wide, empty, and spacious, and so can continue to effortlessly include all your hearing-ness and your seeing-ness, your body-ness and your breathing-ness, your feeling-ness and your thinking-ness. Rest a while in the *awareness of that awareness* that sheds its light on all your experience right now, even as it includes and allows all things to be as they are. It might be said that we began by becoming one with the total mudra of the sitting body, and end by becoming one with the total mudra of this moment of being.

10. Your awareness may now be very open and expanded, as well as more integrated. It may illuminate and reflect the subtlest gestures of appearance: the least flicker of the environment, the

least flicker or wash of our psychic states, supportive and resistant energies of mind, the finest grain in the paper of reality. It may disappear in itself like water in water. As awareness expands, empties, and detaches in this way, it melts the glue that binds the knots of our fixations. As the knots release, the fabric of the mind may be stretched thin enough that light begins to shine through the fabric itself with a sense of great spaciousness. That spaciousness may begin to efface all the mind's ideas of being or not-being. And that which is beyond words discloses itself. What is all this? That is not a question needing to be answered. It just represents our intent and open availability to being. Relax there.

11. When and as you conclude the exercise, allow your awareness to humbly ground itself by just enjoying the natural rise and fall of your breath, and the simplicity of the present moment.

The Temple of
the Body

*D*eep meditation traditions have emerged in many cultures and have employed many postures. From the standpoint of mudra, there are deep antecedents that gave birth to the cross-legged lotus postures that emerged in India, and reasons why they are still so precisely taught and used in Buddhist practice. Their grounding, stability, alignment, and openness served the needs of the long-sitting body, while encouraging a balanced and relaxed alertness, an openness of the breath and the heart, and the optimum flow of *pranic* energies.

Of course, for many of us, especially if we come to practice later in life, the lotus position is difficult to impossible, and may only contribute to tension and distraction. For those who are challenged, but willing, it is possible to learn to overcome many of the obstacles, and, with the right instruction, still assume a modified cross-legged position that confers many of the same benefits of stability, upright alignment, and—believe it or not—comfort. For others, a different position may be adopted—supported kneeling, or sitting upright in a chair—that still incorporates the important principles of groundedness, upright alignment, and openness.

This next practice comes from a lifetime of experience inhabiting and contemplating the lotus sitting posture; and from recognizing the interrelation and correlation between the elements of the body's posture and the elements of a sound, integrated, and open state of mind—such that the sitting body itself serves as an ever available step-by-step manual and reference guide for meditation practice. Hence, I originally called this practice: "Reading Your Buddha Body." Though the lotus posture is especially felicitous for this exercise, and is its original reference, its principles can and should be applied, and its value satisfactorily derived, from any upright posture. This practice is not just a meditation aid; it is a reconstitution of our mind-body integrity and reciprocity—that is, of our character and our psychological health. This is not an otherworldly practice. As before, I encourage you to try practicing this with open eyes for its full integrative benefit.

1. Our *humanity* springs from our *humus,* our soil; and this is the treasure of our *humility:* the willingness and capacity to return to our ground. To sit on the Earth, to be established in our *ground* and in our *root,* is the foundation of all else that may emerge from us. The triangular lotus posture gives us lots of ground to sit on, and lots of room to plant roots. When Buddha called on the Earth to witness his enlightenment, his backside and the Earth already knew each other well.

    The experience of *ground* is archetypal to our bodies and to our psyches (though our modern mind and culture do a huge job of casting it off). Ultimately, our ground is our being. For Being *is* Ground. And being is grounded in itself, and in all its manifestations. Hence, to sit on our ground is a gift of being. To stand on the ground is equally so, if we can keep our attention there.

    That is why it is so supportive, in any posture, to draw our attention down to the ground floor of the body, where we may experience our *groundedness.* As we establish ourselves in groundedness, we can take mantric support from holding in our being the word *grounded.* Groundedness is hard to describe, but we know it when we feel it, both in our bodies and in our souls/psyches. It enables our presence, our integrity, and our vastness. It is a basket that holds the sky.

As we contemplate internally the image of the sitting Buddha body—whatever our sitting position—we take the time we need to establish our felt sense of ground. That itself is the first antidote to the distracting tyranny of the mind. And it is like entering the ground floor of a temple, the temple of the body. As we enter a temple, it calls to us with a sense of greater presence, and it calls us to *be* present. We may even bow to the ground on entry.

This is also like entering a ceremonial tea house (or, for that matter, a stone lodge). The door is low, so all, rich or poor, "nobility" or "commoners," must bow low in the same way on entry. But once inside, we sit up straight, with poise, and rest in rapt attention to each graceful and refined movement of the ceremonial dance of tea. Then we receive the gift of tea with both hands. We all enter as "commoners," but once inside, we are all "nobility."

2. Now that we have entered and established our ground, the second feature of the lotus posture is its stability. We have established broad balance, and we don't have to wobble over time. We may hold the mantra *stable* as we take time to establish our own inner sense of stability, whether or not our physical base is more broad or more narrow. This stability of body is ultimately, of course, a stability of mind, and a stability of being.

3. Having established our ground and our stability, we raise our attention to our dynamic center of body energy and balance in the lower abdomen, just below the navel. This is the deep breathing center known as the *hara* in Zen arts, the *dan tian* in qigong, or the "vase" in some tantric practices. Resting our attention here, we may hold the supportive mantra *centered,* allowing time for the felt sense of centeredness to become real to us. All manner of phenomena, inner and outer, may call to us without disturbing our sense of centered presence or essential self, or our stable attention that rests at center—and which, at

this point, cannot easily be pushed over, abandoned, or under-mined. This is not a narrow "circling of the wagons." Ultimately, being is centered in being.

4. From this lower foundation, or pyramid, of ground, stability, and center, we now bring our attention to the uprightness of the body. We acknowledge and allow our full and extended upright stature, from the gentle supportive curve of the lumbar spine and up along the whole natural alignment and extension of the spine, to the slight relaxation of the chin, and up to the gentle energetic and postural lift of the crown of the head to the sky. (This whole upright alignment of posture is enabled by a slight forward tilt of the pelvis, such that our sitz bones are not rolling back; rather, we feel the full weight of our erect body coming down just on the front side of the sitz bones. A sitting cushion that is raised in the back helps this alignment—and the comfort of our posture.)

The accumulated physical stresses of life, psycho-emotional messages, and gravity itself, may cause us to shrink, and to adopt postures that don't express or accommodate our full innate stat-ure. But there is an upright core of unobstructed physical and psychic energy that wishes to arise to its full stature. We can consciously enable this as we sit in the mudra of *uprightness,* and take additional support from the mantra *upright.* This helps us to restore our bodies and our psyches to their fuller stature, or, we might also say, to the *natural dignity* of our presence. This natural dignity derives from a deeper level than that of our ego's wounds or pretensions. It is the inherent dignity of being, with which we can face into our experience, and with which we can face into the world.

5. Our upright human posture means our most vulnerable aspect is exposed to the world, not facing downward. As humans, we are equipped with the capacity and potential skillfulness to con-duct ourselves in the world in a way that physically protects our

vulnerability, while also honoring it (in ourselves and others), and learning from, growing with, and connecting with it. But our earliest and ongoing developmental wounds (culturally, historically, and personally) have also taught us to protect ourselves through our instinctive defensiveness and aggression, our shutting down, and even the demonizing of our own vulnerability and, with it, our capacity for genuine reciprocity.

Now, in our upright exposure, we have come to the region of the heart and the upper chest, and we must integrate the challenge of our vulnerability and openness. Whereas in our less developed stages of experience we may have had to compromise our openness, now we have come to this openness with the integrative foundation of our felt and cognitive experience of our true groundedness, stability, centeredness, and backbone of innate dignity.

With this team behind us, we have a basis for resting in the temple of the heart with the mantra *open*. We take the time we need to process the fears and objections of the mind and the emotions, while continually coming back to the felt sense and capacity for openness with regard to our arising inner and outer experience. We are tutoring our capacity for allowing both our *feeling* and our *awareness*—in both their active and their receptive aspects—to spread out into the open field. This is to say that this openness will begin to have the force of our love behind it, as well as its receptive and non-reactive availability to things as they are.

This, then, is also our tonglen moment, the empowering of our *giving and receiving*. For our openness is not a static or passive quality. It is inseparable from the breathing flow of give and take. We are not only open, but permeable. The breath expresses our reciprocity and the permeability of inner and outer. As heart and lungs begin to find and resonate with each other, we begin to inhabit our full capacity for exchange with the subjects and objects of our experience, and we surrender our pose of separateness and the fixations that support it. The in-breath and out-breath constitute our full availability to experience. An essential welcome follows along on the in-breath; an essential blessing follows along on the out-breath. Breath by breath, we are nourished; and breath by breath, we nourish. This allows for the blossoming of our love and our compassion.

We have begun by holding the mantra, *open,* at the heart. (If we need the extra support initially, we can hold the mantra *safe.*) Now, also, breath by breath, we can surrender with the mantra *permeable;* or even *allow;* or *receive and bless;* or *love.*

6. There is by now a naturally growing integration of these many domains of our experience. We are allowing previously distant or discordant aspects of ourselves to join together in an integral experience of being. This integration is also expressed in the lotus mudra in the intertwining of our legs, and in the bringing to center of our farthest parts—our feet to our base, and our hands nested close by in our laps. This is palpably experienced as we sit in that posture, reinforcing what we already experience as the growing integration of mind, body, and emotion—the integration of our ground, our center, our expanse, and our parts. In any posture, however, we can sit with our whole felt sense of integration, sealed and encouraged with the mantra *integrated.* The seal of this experience helps to anchor it as a felt sense of integrated self in our daily life.

7. We can return to each floor of our body temple at any time to nourish or strengthen the affiliated quality of being. Or if we are having difficulty accessing the felt sense of a specific quality, we can return to take more time integrating at the prior level, since they support each other in ascending sequence. In time, the structure, the words, and the mantras may all fade from distinction in consciousness, because we are simply sitting in our open and integrated presence—a presence that incorporates all these dimensions of being.

But we can only be said to *experience* all these dimensions of body and mind—ground, stability, center, stature, openness, and so on—because their experience arises in our *awareness*. Awareness is the light and the menstruum of all experience—inner and outer, high and low. So now again we may appreciate the nature of awareness itself, with which we are one, as we raise our attention to the third eye center with the mantra *aware*. Our awareness is the lamp that impartially illumines whatever arises in reality, whether perceived as experienced within our bodies, outside our bodies, or beyond the distinctions of mind and body. As in the previous meditation, we are now resting *in* and *as* the experience of *awareness itself* that is innately all inclusive of all arising experience and content.

8. As the line between awareness and its objects fades, we resolve to that unified field of transparency; and our psychic focus may naturally rise above the crown to rest in the self-dissolving temple of transparency. There is a shining. With our fading self-consciousness we can mutter the mantra *transparent*. But who's listening?

As lofty as all this sounds, it can all proceed in a very grounded and naturally present state. However, if your attention begins to feel over-expanded or spacey, always conclude by dropping any specialness and bringing your attention to the ordinary experience of your ground, your body, your breath, and the humble simplicity of each moment.

Dimensions
of Transparency

*V*ajrayana Buddhism often refers to the five *Dhyani* Buddhas, or Wisdom Buddhas, primordial aspects of the enlightened mind. These five Buddhas are often portrayed on a "medicine wheel" mandala of four directions and a center. And they are sometimes employed—like the enneagram—to designate fundamental spiritual and personality types and families, each with distinguishing characteristics of enlightenment and ignorance.

My primary interest in them, however, is in how they have arisen for me as archetypes and as active dimensions of the integral functions of transparency, or enlightened mind. And each also has a distinguishing hand mudra, which is profound in its mind/body effect. As I sit with them in my practice, as I become them, they each provide a template by which my consciousness can clarify itself in their light and assume their dimension. As my inner circuitry aligns itself with each archetypal dimension of being, I feel the allowed shift in consciousness in real time. In my own meditation, after having spent time with integrating at the levels of the body temple, or engaging in whatever other meditation I may be doing, I'll often conclude my sitting time actively embracing and exercising the five dimensions as a reinforcement and attunement of my dharma practice.

Please bear in mind that I am not attempting to bring any scholarly exposition to this matter, or even any technical orthodoxy in my presentation of the five wisdoms. I am simply sharing my own practice that I have adopted and adapted from my own instincts and interpretations, from which others have received benefit, and which I have not seen spoken of elsewhere.

And please remember that though in practice they can become a living presence, each of these Buddhas is also just an ideal. We needn't regard these Buddhas, or this practice, as a mirror by which to judge ourselves, or by which to receive a pass, fail, or A+. They are training opportunities. In their generosity, these five Buddhas can invite us up to their level or meet us wherever we are, compassionately informing and supporting us through our baby steps with endless patience—and with knowledge of who we really are. So we can take appropriate benefit from this practice at any time.

1. The Buddha of the Center, known as *Vairochana* Buddha, is the Buddha of the primordial spaciousness of being. At the primordial level of reality, all is transparently unobstructed. We might say he is the Buddha of inexhaustible non-exclusiveness, without any basis for the duality or reactivity of our projective minds. Hence, this dimension of our transparency rests with equanimity and openness at the heart of all arising form, including the subtlest contents of our own minds.

    This is not exactly my everyday state of mind. But as I sit as each Buddha, my intention—along with the mudra—allows me to become more coherent with, and to amplify, my experience of integrating that particular dimension of consciousness. As I have said, it seems to create a wiring—an inner circuitry—of integrity and wholeness that, in this case, increases my capacity to remain in non-reactive availability to the whole field of consciousness, including whatever dire messaging my mind may have been bombarding me with earlier.

    It is as if I've become an infinitely small and empty point in space—like a neutrino, that can pass through all other atomic structures—too small to be affected even by the atomic structure of a thought, yet consequently of spacious presence. Hence this is the dimension of spaciousness not so much from the *expansiveness* of space, but from the absence of any reactivity that could *interfere* with spaciousness. It is rather like the empty and all accommodating space of the zero-point field.

The mudra associated with this Buddha is one I played with and found awkward, and modified at first, but which I now appreciate as an almost miraculous rewiring that instantly converts my state of mind. In this mudra, the thumb and first finger of each hand touch. Then, with hands at right angles—the left hand horizontal and the right hand vertical and just above—the tips of both touching fingers are brought together and all four touch, hands held in front of the heart. I often feel like the mudra connection shuts off my mind and does all the work for me.

2. Any reactivity on the part of our minds—any projection, choosing, or judging things to be this or that—will prejudice and compromise the full extent and clarity of our awareness; for it replaces a mirror-like awareness with one that shades, pulls back from, or deflects around the edges of some experiences while highlighting others. In impartial spaciousness, there is nothing to compromise either the vastness or the faithful mirror-like illumination of awareness. Hence, awareness may naturally extend to all things, to all corners, and to all domains. This is the realm of *Akshobya* Buddha.

    In this dimension of transparency, awareness may illuminate the widest outward-moving peripheral spread of the attention, along with the most intimate mote of dust before us. The associated mudra has the left palm upturned in the lap with the right palm draped over the right knee, touching (either physically or energetically) the ground. I think of this as my left hand open to the universe, and my right hand connecting to the communication grid of the whole planet. And I let my vast awareness extend across heaven and earth.

3. Without the darkness of reactivity, and with the open light of awareness, the inherent blessing energy of the nature of being shines through in its own fullness. This is the natural abundance or gift of being that may now nourish us and overflow us. This is *Ratnasambhava* Buddha, the gift-giving or wish-fulfilling Buddha. And this is the inherent generosity and gift-giving aspect of the transparent mind. It expresses as the generosity of our attention, the generosity of our heart, in material generosity, and in the generosity of each incidental act of living or relationship. We rest with the left hand still upturned in our laps, but now with the right hand also upturned over the knee, and extending itself forward, or draped slightly backward over the knee, in the gesture of giving everything away. It is not a static gesture. We feel in our open awareness, in our heart, and in our extended palm, the energy of giving.

4. Our generous presence, our vast awareness, and our non-reactive equality and spaciousness of seeing cannot help but take in all the realms of light and dark, the joys and sufferings of sentient beings. And we cannot but hold them all in our heart with absolute compassionate intent. Hence, as both hands now nest upturned in our lap, palm in palm, we sit as the unobstructed sun of compassion, the *Amitabha* Buddha. I sometimes experience in my nesting hands that I am holding a great sun of compassion at my center, and that it is radiating out with my awareness throughout the universe. Each of these dimensions, and their mudras, are inviting us to absorb in them and become one with them for a while.

5. As we allow and encompass these innate transparent domains of our own being—our non-reactive and spacious presence, our vast and intimate awareness, our generosity of outlook and behavior, and our compassion—we continue to integrate these into our neural circuitry, reconditioning brain, body, and heart. And we are at last becoming able to act skillfully in the world,

with wisdom, equanimity, and love. This is the dimension of *Amoghasiddhi,* the Buddha of Right Action. We have dropped the illusions and compulsions of control, but are capable of optimal participation, responding with instinctive appropriateness to circumstances and to the needs of others, and trusting in the natural unfolding of reality, in which we are compassionate co-creators.

Where the River Widens

Never be afraid to go there—where the river widens.
Once you thought only the bank
was a suitable home for a creature like you.
If asked about the world, you would explain,
"It is a dry place. Grass is sleek
and sharp, bark is rough, dirt crumbles.
Hope is sky. One picks his way there among distinct
forms and shadows."

Now the taste of the water is
in some ways like your first taste, the current of excitement
like your first excitement, the cool on
your skin, the buoyancy—sometimes your feet
touched bottom, increasingly not.

You allowed it, still thinking, "My life on
the bank controls this. I will tell the others. It is good."
But now it is too late to talk. You are midstream. The river
has taken you. You are an unfolding of that current,
not a body with a self. Every moment you are
descending. Every moment you are rising in another world.
You are the soft ribbon of life that can breathe anywhere.

Here, where the river widens, everything widens. Everything calls.
There is no end to this widening. This can never again
be your life. Do not be afraid to go there.

Epilogue

On the window ledge over my kitchen sink sits a large Chinese Buddhist statue of Guanyin, the goddess of compassion. She is beautiful and very heavy. I lugged her all over China with me in the late nineties, from north to south, before finally hauling her home. She was a joyous weight. She reminds me of the steady flow of compassion from "on high," which is also our own reality.

In the early 2000s, my son Josiah visited Sarajevo. He brought back a chipped piece of tan brick. The brick came to sit in Guanyin's lap. It had been splintered from a church—or a mosque, I don't remember— that had received heavy shelling or machine gun fire during the civil war. The heartbreak of that conflict has receded in our minds now, to be replaced by all the subsequent heartbreaks. I was grateful that my son had stopped to pick up that brick and bring it home for Guanyin. Together they have become for me "the altar of everything."

"The altar of everything" is an altar to our own necessary work: to the compassionate embrace of the suffering of this world. After all, the catalog of current and past warfare, genocides, and atrocities that occur far and near, and in our own history, are all extreme instances of the deluded dynamic of separateness and greed that characterizes our human experience. The fundamental solidification of a self and self-interest, so innocently and necessarily begun (and so often complicated and fixated by trauma), augmented by our growing virtual structures of identity, attachment, aversion, and denial, turns our human experience upside down, and turns us away from the direction of our freedom.

When I look at Guanyin on my counter, I see she is holding in her lap the suffering of the world captured in that little piece of brick. Guanyin is said to have ears that enable her to listen to all the suffering of the world, a heart that can hold it all, and the willingness to appear in any form that will help alleviate suffering. This capacity is founded in her realization of "emptiness." Not an emptiness, we have learned, that is the nihilistic denial of experience or of suffering. Rather, it is emptiness that is empty of "story" or drama, empty of projection or reification, and empty of reactivity. It is this emptiness that leaves the heart the *maximum space* with which to embrace experience without flinching, and thus be able to receive and to bless.

Guanyin, of course, represents a potential capacity within human beings. It is a capacity that the suffering of the world is asking of us; not only because *it* needs it of *us,* but also because *we* need it of *ourselves.* To hear anyone speak these days, our hearts have never been more challenged. We stand in the world at the heart of paradox, with one foot in the beauty that we are, and one foot in the sorrow. And that must ever be the crucible of our capacity to love. To persist as love despite all evidence to the contrary.

This paradox of opposites is true not only for our confrontation with the world, but also for the confrontation with our own lives. Heroes or villains, we never drop our (sometimes unconscious) reference point for beauty or happiness, even while having to assimilate the circumstances of suffering or sorrow. But our representations of happiness and suffering occur, and are sustained in, the reified realm of our thinking— where they are often delusive; where they can never be resolved, only projected. And in which we can never truly know ourselves or others. Thus, the canvas of oppression and exploitation that is stretched across the planet—the patterns of hierarchy, power, greed, self-interest, and all the destructive and exclusive ambitions of "me and mine" that we know politically, economically, socially, and even ecologically—is only the "exploded" image of the self-system that we ourselves must negotiate and awaken to in each aspect of our own lives.

If I am not conscious enough to recognize this dynamic, and to take responsibility for it, it will always turn toxic within me, becoming, in fact, what Buddhism refers to as the three poisons: greed, anger (or hatred), and ignorance, ignorance even of my own relationship to life. In its ultimately toxic or perverted form, I can even maintain that the resolution of my condition can be obtained by the suffering or exploitation of others; or even that the elimination of a whole population of people will restore me to happiness. In this sense, the aspiration to eliminate a group of people is not, at the deepest core, different from the aspiration to love. It is our heart's true inner aspiration for an inexhaustible non-exclusiveness, for felicity and love, manifesting tragically in toxic and deluded form.

The powerful *samsaric* consequences (i.e., our seeming worldly and historical realities) are all created and sustained by the activity of projection and delusion, fueled by the "for-itself." The sage Longchenpa characterizes our delusions as "tying space into knots." There is an inherent freedom and natural reciprocity in the spontaneous impermanence and flow of life in both *awareness* and *experience*. But we tie that spacious reality into the knots of our fixated projections, beliefs, and separative categories, creating a new fictitious "literal" reality.

The reverse process of responsibility always entails the re-owning of our projections and of our subjective experience, which takes the form of self-honesty and self-insight in the moment. This is a level of prefrontal development available to our species, but one which requires a supportive level of nurturance and safety, and thus is widely inhibited by all levels of cultural or familial trauma. All inner growth begins when we perceive self-honesty as contributing to our genuine freedom, not to our doom. Then, as Zen says, the strength of our capacity to doubt all projection is married to the strength of our ultimate faith. Then we may *see through* the understandable conviction—derived both from the paradox of dualism and from the traumas of childhood—that "things as they are" and "I as I am" are not sufficient for my well-being. For it is, in fact, from the inherent sufficiency and trust in both that the process of healing derives.

That is why our availability to awakening can be fostered—as in the True Heart, True Mind process—by our faith in speaking the truth of *ourselves* as we perceive it, but fused with a sincere intention and openness to the actual truth of things beyond our projection. This is truly to "take refuge" in things as they are, which is where we may discover that things as they are—an awake and intimate universe—hold the true key to the resolution of our suffering.

In this regard, allow me to share one last "ordinary" experience that occurred during one of my evening groups, some years after the last experience recorded at the end of part one. On this occasion I was participating as one of an even number of people doing a dyad process together. I should say, by way of context, that there is a recognized boundary to be negotiated between the role of a group facilitator—holding the container—and also being present as one's whole self, modeling mutuality and honest self-awareness as appropriate. I say "negotiated," because I prefer that boundary to breathe with a genuine and mindful balance; both sides are of service to the group. It is always a moment of discernment. But it will affect when and how I disclose my own process.

At that time, I was feeling some distress over a number of personal issues and self-doubts that were arising. Did I want to introduce my own doubts or confusion into the evening? And was it for the sake of the group or my own ego that I hesitated? I couldn't abide or subscribe to the energy of participating but not being real. I opted again for genuine participation; the simple truth and my willingness to speak it within the boundaried structure of the communication process. That decision is actually more important than the content. For content is always changing and relative, while straightforward honesty and faith is fundamental. So I began straightforwardly to get across to my dyad partner the truth of what I was experiencing.

Within a few sentences, I began to feel carried along by something else, as if it were speaking through me. It was *truth itself*—a stream of transparent reality that was one with, and superseded, the relative truth that I was communicating. As I continued speaking that relative truth—that circumstantial truth—some part of me realized "Oh my God, it's the *full father shift*" (see the chapter titled "I and My Father Are One"). The stream of being, flowing into the world from and as the Original Source, was all that was present in the communication of my worldly distress; and I was simply one with it. The distress dissolved, and I was left with a coherence that was inwardly joyful.

It was a valuable lesson and reminder for me. For I can still be quite subject to the mechanisms of ego; and, at their fiercest, a grave self-doubt. But at times I receive reassurance that it is all "part of the job" of being human. As if I am a double agent. "Go in there, become a local. Forget who you are. Take notes. Report back." But then, in moments of clarity, I spill the beans on "the country" that sent me. And though I have honed my recognition of my "double agent" status over time, it is essentially true for all of us.

Most importantly, I am continually reinspired by the power of truth—not dogma, but the truth of two or more people sitting across from each other, heart to heart, doing the work of becoming present to each other, and being completely vulnerable to the way things are. That is the Presence of which it is said that when two or more people are gathered on its behalf, "I am there."

It is obvious that our human species, still living out a stressful, survivalist, dog-eat-dog side of our primitive nervous and hormonal systems—inflamed with wounded and deranged egos, and doing great damage to each other—has not had, by and large, the wholesome luxury or safety of coming together in this way and recognizing each other in mutual presence, aside from sometimes within our small groups. We have moments of awakening at the heart but are not able to rest or remain coherent there. Even so, the teachings of the heart continue to call to us. We must bring to bear, and live with, an astute intelligence and compassion with regard to our ignorance and the consequences that seem to follow. We are cells of one body that, one by one, become activated and tutored in making the decision to "persist as love despite all evidence to the contrary."

Today, the individual practices that encourage our coherence, and the clarification of our minds and our hearts—a reengagement with the reciprocity and intimacy that reflect the true nature of our being— must be matched by our practice in community as well. And that also demands of us the real work of reciprocity, of authentic communication, and of *presence* together, face to face and heart to heart. And it demands of us as well that mutual vulnerability that leaves space for the necessary reconsideration of our lives.

Gandhi once said, to paraphrase: My life's work isn't to 'free India'; my life's work is to live in spiritual truth with God, and this happens to be how I do it. Gandhi's genius and unique power was to carry the ethos of integrity, transparency, and reciprocity into all his actions. When our lives become the path, we address in our own way the twin principles of integrity (the "in-itself") and compassion (the "for-others"); and we do whatever work our heart knows is required. And there are people all around us, both hidden and not so hidden, both conscious and not so conscious, doing their genuine part.

I offer this book to support, to underscore, and to reinvigorate our transcendent understanding and our immanent commitment to the practical realization of our innate oneness and our inherent freedom. And so that we may uphold, in the face of all of the challenges that today and tomorrow will bring us—whether through our own day's affairs or the morning news—our faith, integrity, and compassion; and the reciprocity so necessary if we are to face each other and face together into this next moment, and into this next era, so fraught with new delusions and new possibilities.

So as I sit here across from you now, it is not from any further desire to "tell you" anything, but to listen together to what our silence tells us, while not disowning ourselves or the voice that speaks us. Thank you for allowing me to tell so much of my own story. And there is no greater pleasure for me now than to be able to hear yours.

I confess I also have a great love for trees, and for forest paths; for rocks and cliff sides; for the lone pine or cactus growing on the high desert ledge; for flowing streams; for surf; for the coral outcrop on which I first conceived this book. For the reed grass growing on the great marshes. For me they are numinous doorways into the infinite. But I confess also and most of all, here in the growing shadow of the day, my love for the unique sparkle in your own eyes. They carry me home.

After the April Retreat

This old monk's no good at this.
He just wants to raise acorns.
And if your pigs are hungry,
well—all right—they're free.

Spring morning drizzle
puts a shine on autumn's leaves.
I walk my boggy woods
clearing the trails
of winter's depredations.
Each time I never know
if I'll emerge again.

We have talked of meeting
a long time. Your
voice called to me like a rustle
of satin in the leaves.

Now that I have paused
in the deep woods,
sitting on a bit of high ground
under the swamp maples,
it seems we have enough right here,
silent as the moss,
to keep us busy for lifetimes.

Useful Terms

*T*he following meanings, while not comprehensive, are included here to help guide you through the stories and discussions contained in this book.

Arising content: Whatever arises in thought or perception

The Beatitudes: Sayings of Jesus recounted in the Sermon on the Mount in the Gospel of Matthew and in the Sermon on the Plain in the Gospel of Luke

Bodhicitta: In Buddhism, an individual moral commitment to awakening and to service; the essential activity of love and awakening in reality itself

Bodhisattva: In Buddhism, accomplished beings whose lives and activity are founded on bodhicitta; also, any of us, when bodhicitta awakens in us or moves us

Buddha-mind: The true, open, and luminous non-dual nature of consciousness

Buddha-nature: Our underlying nature, one with conscious loving presence, that can become actualized and experienced through practice

Buddhism: A vast tradition of many schools of philosophy, psychology, and spiritual practice deriving from Gautama Buddha's enlightened insights and teachings in the fifth and sixth centuries BCE

Ch'an: Chinese Buddhist lineages founded on meditation and direct transmission, from which Japanese Zen derives

Dharma: Buddhist teachings on the nature of reality and the path of realization

Dharmadhatu: In Buddhism, the fundamental non-dual space of being and all phenomena

Dharmata: In Buddhism, the intrinsic nature, or true essence of things, outside of language

Dyad: A two-person process; a structured communication exercise

Ein Sof: In the Kabbalah, the infinite aspect of God, or Reality, beyond all ideas or categories

FLINCH response: Acronym for Failure to Love Into the Next Conscious Happening; the tendency to contract away from experience; replacing intimacy, presence, and compassion with avoidance, judgment, or control

The Four Noble Truths: Four primary teachings of the Buddha on the nature of suffering and the release of suffering

God: Referred to here as the fundamental infinite and intimate nature of reality; an ultimate Conscious Loving Presence

Holographic reality: Reality as a projection of the Dharmadhatu, or God's Infinite Mind

Inexhaustible non-exclusiveness: Another term for the non-dual, infinite, and interpenetrating nature of reality

Interoception: The faculty of attention that can tune into the body and sense it inwardly

Karma: In Buddhism, conscious act; the principle of cause and effect: how our perceptions, intentions, and choices in this moment contribute to a structure of reality that determines our perceptions and choices in the next moment, and also invites a balancing feedback from that reality

Koan: In Zen and Ch'an Buddhism, a paradoxical story, question, or statement posed to provoke enlightenment

The Lord's Prayer: A prayer found in the New Testament in which Jesus responds to his disciples' question of how they should pray

Mantra: A word or phrase repeated to aid in meditation

Mother Lode: The source of treasure; the main vein of ore; a principal and rich source

Mudra: A ritual gesture or pose

Nirvana: The coming to rest of the ego's dualistic reality and consequent suffering

The Noble Eightfold Path: The Buddha's sequel to the Four Noble Truths; the path of liberation

Non-duality: The nature of reality as an intimate, spontaneous, and integral wholeness of being that is paradoxical and unfathomable to the mind's tendency to perceive everything in terms of separation, boundary, contrast, and opposition; a unifying mode of perception beyond all categories

Qigong: A modern term for the ancient Chinese science of energy flow, harmony, and cultivation, derived initially from Taoist practice

Reify: To assign literal reality to that which is only appearance, thought, projection, or a category of the mind; to attribute separateness, solidity, and permanence to things or thoughts, rather than seeing them as expressions of a greater interdependent whole

Rigpa: In Tibetan Buddhism, primordial wakefulness; pristine awareness and presence

Rigpa-tsal: The radiant and creative energy of *rigpa,* from which appearance arises

Samantabhadra: In Vajrayana Buddhism, the personified representation of primordial awareness or Buddha-nature

Samantabhadri: In Vajrayana Buddhism, the personification of primordial creativity, manifestation, and appearance; the beloved of Samantabhadra

Samsara: The endless cycle of relativity and suffering fueled by dualistic perceptions, intentions, and choices

Sangha: In Buddhism, community of practice

Shikan taza: "Just sitting," a form of meditation in Japanese Zen

Taoism: The cumulative naturalistic wisdom tradition of ancient China, addressing the way of harmony between the underlying unity and the creative polarities of life, and strongly influencing Chinese philosophy, religion, ethics, science, art, and medicine

Tonglen: In Buddhism, compassionate meditation in which we breathe in another's suffering and send back love and healing on the outbreath

The True Heart, True Mind Intensive: A profound and intensive retreat process that combines dyad communication with contemplative inquiry on a question such as "Who am I?" promoting both self-integration and awakening; also known as the Enlightenment Intensive

The virtual world: The reality that we perceive as a construct of our mental representations and projections

The wisdom traditions: All our spiritual traditions collectively that point us toward a more unified and loving perception of reality

Zen: Japanese lineages of Buddhism, widely associated with meditation and direct experience, and sometimes spontaneous and paradoxical teaching; the word and the tradition derive from the Chinese *ch'an* and the Sanskrit *dhyana,* or meditation

Index

BOOKS OF RELATED INTEREST

Yoga Nidra Meditation
The Sleep of the Sages
by Pierre Bonnasse

The Dharma Method
7 Daily Steps to Spiritual Advancement
by Simon Chokoisky

Tibetan Yoga
Principles and Practices
by Ian A. Baker
Foreword by Bhakha Tulku Pema Rigdzin Rinpoche

Embodying the Mystery
Somatic Wisdom for Emotional, Energetic, and Spiritual Awakening
by Richard Strozzi-Heckler

Being Nature
A Down-to-Earth Guide to the Four Foundations of Mindfulness
by Wes Nisker
Foreword by Jack Kornfield

The Heart of Yoga
Developing a Personal Practice
by T. K. V. Desikachar

The Yoga-Sūtra of Patañjali
A New Translation and Commentary
by Georg Feuerstein, Ph.D.

Kriya Yoga for Self-Discovery
Practices for Deep States of Meditation
by Keith G. Lowenstein, M.D.
With Andrea J. Lett, M.A.

INNER TRADITIONS • BEAR & COMPANY
P.O. Box 388
Rochester, VT 05767
1-800-246-8648
www.InnerTraditions.com
Or contact your local bookseller